The
Hidden
Mission
Field

Caring for the Widow and Orphan in the 21st Century

Theresa McKenna

WINEPRESS WP PUBLISHING

ISBN 1-57921-171-2
Library of Congress Catalog Card Number: 98-89461

In my prayers, the Holy Spirit has given me a vision of courageous men and women across the nation, pastors and lay leaders from every denomination, standing up, called by God to form an army that will minister to single-parents and their children. For every person whose heart has ever been stirred by this incredible ministry, I humbly dedicate this work.

ACKNOWLEDGEMENTS

Those who know me well will not be surprised to find a reference to gardening on this page. Like putting the plants into the ground, writing this book represents a small part of the entire process. For years, God has had me planning the garden—defining the borders, preparing the beds, amending the soil, and selecting the flowers that I would use. It has taken a long time to complete the preparation.

I want to acknowledge my friends, the Lands, for loving me through the worst time in my life. I also want to thank the special people who helped me with the single-parent ministry at Mercer Island Covenant Church, especially Dan and Sandra Smith. Together, we worked through problems and experienced the joys of seeing a ministry bear abundant fruit. I also want to thank my colleague Pastor David Jobe for the encouragement and affirmation, without which the past couple of years would have been torture.

Most of all, I want to thank my wonderful daughters, Claire and Meredith, for their steadfast love and for their unfailing belief in me. There has never been a moment that I have not been proud to be their mother.

A wonderful neighbor, an older and wiser lady, once told me that it was good to plant my troubles in the garden. "They always look so much better when they bloom." With the completion of this book, I pray there will be many blossoms from which to choose.

CONTENTS

PART THREE: MINISTRY TO WIDOWS AND ORPHANS

INTRODUCTION

Not long after my divorce, my friend Diana called and related to me that, in her morning prayer, God had told her to share Jeremiah 29:11 with me and that I was to hold on to that verse as evidence of His faithfulness. "For I know the plans I have for you declares the Lord, plans to prosper you and not to harm you, plans to give you hope and a future." I remember that morning very well. I sat on the edge of my bed, with hot tears rolling down my checks. Lots of things were racing through my mind, not the least of them was the sense that I had already been "harmed." There was little hope, and the future looked dismal. "Prosperity" was simply a joke. I was struggling for mere survival.

In my personal pity party that morning, it seemed to me that all of my life I had struggled. I was born to an unwed mother at a time when there was not yet acceptability but only shame and humiliation. My stepfather hated me, and I loathed him in return. I felt abandoned by my mother, even though she married out of what she considered to be my best interest. My profoundly dysfunctional childhood experiences served to propel me into an equally dysfunctional marriage. It wasn't until after my husband left with one of my best friends that I found the Lord. It felt like I was being punished.

As I look back upon it now, I can clearly see the hand of God. He was not punishing me. He would not even have wished me to endure the pain, because He loves me and He would not want me to be harmed. Only good and perfect things come from God. It is because we live in a fallen world that those other things happened—some by my choices, some by others'. But by allowing the many struggles in my life, God uniquely prepared me for a ministry to single-parent families.

I have a tender heart for unwed mothers. I know the humiliation and pain of a divorce. I understand firsthand the sense of abandonment by a parent—both in my own situation and by observing my children. I know that God allowed me to experience those struggles so that I would have a passion for a ministry that He considers very important.

People often tell me that my passion for single-parent family ministry creeps into my conversations within a few minutes, whether I am talking to friends or to total strangers. It's true. I am passionate about it, not only because I have been a single parent for so long and I know firsthand how hard it is, or because I know that God has called me to this ministry, I am passionate about single-parent family ministry because I am passionate about the Great Commission. We are called to love and minister to everyone who does not yet know Jesus Christ. We are to look for the stranger who does not know the gospel and share it with him. Yet, I am deeply concerned that the church rarely considers single-parent families when they consider their outreach ministry. It breaks my heart because I wonder how long we in the church can continue to ignore this huge but hidden mission field. I wonder how long God will be patient with us as we ignore the cries of the modern-day widows and orphans—single-parent families.

Modern Widows and Orphans

1

SINGLE PARENTS IN THE LATE TWENTIETH CENTURY

WHEN ALISON WALKED into my office, she already knew I was her friend. We had met each other years earlier when our oldest children were in kindergarten together. We attended our church's first attempt at single-parent family ministry in the "Single Again" Sunday-school class. But a lot had changed since that time. I had sold my business when I felt God calling me into a full-time ministry to single-parent families. After a few years in seminary, I was beginning my internship on staff at our church.

Things had not gone well for Alison. She had remarried and, after four years, divorced again, following the birth of her daughter. Her husband, whom she had met at church, turned out to be physically abusive. As she walked into my office, I did a mental survey of the issues I knew about: she had a nine-year-old son from her first marriage, a ten-month-old baby, no job, serious health problems, bills to pay, and a very controlling ex-husband who was doing his best to spread vicious rumors throughout the community.

Alison knew I was her friend, but I could tell by the look in her eyes that she didn't know exactly what to expect of me in my new role. The months of humiliation and stress registered on every muscle in her face. I was happy just to see her. She couldn't know that I didn't feel any need to judge her.

I believe that God can redeem every circumstance, and I knew from personal experience that a painful divorce can be a spiritual dichotomy. On one hand, God hates divorce. He hates the breaking of the covenant between two people. He hates what precedes the actual dissolution decree: the anger, the betrayal, the lack of willingness to love one's mate as Christ loves us. And God hates what happens after the divorce. He hates the ripping apart of a family. He hates seeing lives destroyed, and He hates that Satan appears to be winning. On the other hand, God allows those things that allow for us to turn to Him. As the old saying goes, if it doesn't kill us, it makes us stronger. Divorce can make our relationship with Jesus stronger. A divorce completely empties us of ourselves, and that is when Jesus can do the most for us. Alison looked empty.

My only concern was she knew that the church was a safe place for her and her children. As I listened with aches of personal recollection to her plight, I held her daughter and allowed her to play with the telephone on my desk. I promised Alison that we could help her pay some bills and encouraged her when she expressed that no matter what she did, she would continue to be at least three hundred dollars short each month.

"God owns the cattle on a thousand hills, Alison. I'm sure that we can find a way to help you out, especially while you are physically unable to work. Let's not worry yet."

"Thank you," she whispered. "I just can't imagine where I would turn if the church couldn't help me."

I felt good. *This is what ministry is all about,* I thought to myself. *Praise God for allowing me to help other single parents. Praise God that I went through the fire myself so that I know what it feels like to be in her place. Thank you, Lord, that you called me.* I glorified God as I walked into the administrator's office with the benevolence form in my hand.

I had been painfully naïve. The concept that I had of helping this single mom not only did not resonate with Mr. Benton, the administrator, but it also lit up every button on his chest.

"What do you mean by 'ongoing help'?" he said. "We are not a welfare agency, you know."

"Oh, I know," I countered. "But Alison is a single parent who has been a member of this church for a long time. She needs our help until she gets back on her feet. She is behind in her bills, and she has two children to take care of with only a part-time job. This is what it means to provide for the widows and orphans in their distress."

"She's not a widow. She walked out on her husband. Do you want the church to look like it will take care of every woman who walks out on her husband? God hates divorce. Do you remember that from seminary?"

"He beat her! Are you suggesting that she should stay with a man who beats her?"

"She probably provoked him. When they refuse to press charges, that usually means that they know they had something to do with it. Why don't you tell her to go live with her parents until this cools down?"

"Her parents live five hundred miles away. Her son is in the fourth grade. She can't take him out of school. Mr. Benton, there is no justification for a man hitting his wife in the stomach. She had internal bleeding and a cracked rib. I don't want to comment on her unwillingness to press charges, beyond saying that it's my experience that abused people typically fail to press charges out of fear of what could happen next if they do. All I need to know is that Alison is a member of our church. She is a single parent in serious need. Our responsibility is to help her." My eyes were beginning to sting as they often do when I feel myself caught between anger and frustration.

"Our benevolence limit is two hundred and fifty dollars a year. If she has bills that amount to about two hundred and fifty dollars, I'll pay them for her. But that's it. She needs to learn how to stand on her own two feet. I don't believe that we should enable her. If she needs long-term help, then she needs to get on welfare. That's what it's for."

I closed my eyes feeling utterly defeated as I quickly turned and walked out the door to my office. Behind my eyelids tears of frustration were ready to burst through the dam. To my back, I heard him say, "There are consequences to sin, you know."

There are consequences when we do not obey God. Divorce and illegitimacy are the consequences of sin, and I would not suggest that they should be condoned. But they must be forgiven. God has not put sexual sins in a special category that is titled "unforgivable." It is we, in the church, who have tended to harbor unforgivingness for divorce and illegitimacy. God-loving people often say to me that providing ministry to single parents condones their behavior. I don't believe that. I don't condone violent crimes, but I believe in prison ministry.

Although every sin has consequences, not all of them are as obvious as broken families. What about the innocent people who get caught up in the consequences, particularly the children? Regardless of who is at fault, how can we deny ministry to nearly one-third of our nation's families?

Throughout history, wars, plagues, famines, and natural disasters have presented times when the number of single-parent families may have rivaled a rate similar to the one experienced in North America during the late twentieth century. Divorce and illegitimacy are relatively new, in terms of creating huge numbers of single-parent families. Although Americans have always allowed for divorce that is inexpensive enough for the middle class to dissolve its marriages, divorce itself was rare. Between 1910 and 1919, divorce occurred at 4.5 per 1,000 marriages. Each of the world wars disrupted family life and initiated a spike in divorces, as well as a rise in illegitimacy. But immediately after the wars, family life returned to normal, and the divorce and illegitimacy birth rates dropped back to prewar levels.[1]

All that changed in the early 1960s. Two things in particular laid the foundation for my confrontation with the church administrator that afternoon. In 1964, President Lyndon Johnson announced "an unconditional war on poverty" by declaring that that he would enact a fully financed welfare state. He was able to move through Congress some of the most wide-sweeping social legislation since Roosevelt. The "Great Society," as he termed it, would change the face and heart of the nation. The government assumed virtually complete responsibility for the poor and the distressed, often with the blessings of the church. Hubert Humphrey credited clergy support and the formation of IRCAP (Inter-Religious Committee Against Poverty) for the passage of government poverty programs. Key church leaders committed their denominations to back the war on poverty from the pulpit. Praise for the legislation was promptly and frequently voiced by Vatican Radio.[2]

Going far beyond social security, these new programs provided monies under names that conjur up images of embattled Third World countries: Aid to Families with Dependent Children, WIC (Women Infants and Children), HUD (Housing and Urban Development), etc. What typically had been done by family, by caring individuals in community, and most commonly in community churches, suddenly became the purview of the federal government.

By 1971, the government was spending more on welfare than it was on defense.[3] And it did so in spite of the fact that the United States was still heavily involved in the Cold War as well as a war in Southeast Asia. Against the backdrop of the Great Society, the safety net of the church looked anemic and insignificant. Church ministry seemed redundant. Why send out a rowboat when the government was sending out a battleship to do the same work? Abdicating to the magnanimous gestures of Uncle Sam, the mainline and evangelical churches, within a few short years, stepped back and dusted their collective hands of the needy—especially the ones Scripture calls "the widow, the orphan, and the alien" within our own nation.

Simultaneously, the 1960s and 1970s saw a revolution of sexual mores in which love was free and marriage vows were casually rewritten to connote that commitment would last only as long as it felt good. In 1970, California enacted the first no-fault divorce statute. Ten years later, all but two states had followed suit. As a means of personal expression, divorce moved from a rare occurrence to a common phenomenon. When the divorce rate stabilized in the 80s, it was at the highest level among Western nations.[4]

Christian families in America differed little from society at large. Divorce levels among the churched remained neck and neck with the unchurched. Church leaders and theologians sensed a deepening crisis among the church family, a crisis few were prepared to address. Personal and sexual scandals among Christian leaders were prominent in front-page news stories across the country. In individual churches, pastors expressed sorrow and shame. But whole denominations behaved like dogs slinking away with their tails between their legs.

Parachurch ministry found a new cause. In 1977, Dr. James Dobson began his ministry Focus on the Family with the release of the videos entitled *Turn Your Heart toward Home*, a series of filmed speeches about family and family life. About the same time, Bill Gothard began Family Life Conferences.

Within a few short years, there developed a politically polarized debate over the state of the American family, a debate that centered around the use of the term "family values." Political conservatives pointed to abortion, illegitimacy, homosexuality, and irresponsible fathers—"deadbeat dads"—as key indicators of a self-destructive society. Liberals, on the other hand, referred to domestic violence, economic insecurity, and the lack of adequate family support as the key issues affecting the American family.

Neither group spoke much of divorce, for fear of alienating a large constituency of divorced people and for fear of calling attention to the number of divorces within their own leadership. Political conservatism and religious conservatism became virtually indistinguishable. Illegitimacy became synonymous with welfare mothers. Divorced parents were identified with sexual promiscuity, while children of divorce were characterized, at best, as undisciplined and, at worst, as school dropouts and gang members. Although the issue of easy divorce skewed the debate, the single-parent family came to be represented as all that was wrong with American society. Paradoxically, the call to turn the eyes of the church to the restoration of the ideal traditional family has almost certainly been among the issues that has taken the eyes of the church off single parent families.

2

MODERN-DAY WIDOWS AND ORPHANS

Who Are These Single Parents?

OGDEN NASH ONCE said, "A family is a unit composed not only of children, but of men, women, an occasional animal, and the common cold."[1] That would be called a traditional family in today's vernacular; today however, traditional families are less and less in evidence. There are still children, an occasional animal, and perhaps more than the occasional cold, but in over eleven million households, there is absent either a man or a woman who is the mother or father of those children. In fact, over sixteen million children under the age of eighteen live with only one parent. Eighty-seven percent of the time, that parent is their mother.[2]

Today we generally assume that mothers will be awarded custody of their children. However, women receiving custody of their children is a historically recent phenomenon. For centuries, when divorce occurred, mothers had no rights regarding their children, on the grounds that women had no means of taking care of their children. Furthermore, for centuries, mothers regularly died in childbirth. It was commonly assumed that fathers were the more logical choice to maintain custody over their children. The attitude prevailed until the early decades of the twentieth century, when the women's emancipation movement gave women new opportunities. Commercial self-sufficiency, coupled with the medical advances that saved multitudes of women from early death in childbirth, influenced the perception of the courts to place more weight on the nurturing capability of the custodial parent, as opposed to financial capability alone. An assumption was made that mothers did more to bond with their children in the day-to-day nurturing process than did fathers.

Fathers, on the other hand, have been long featured either as harsh, uncaring, rebellion-producing louts or as disassociated workaholics. Their status as primary breadwinner has not conveyed an ability to serve indispensably as a parent. The social climate that produced the women's movement, no-fault divorce, and abortion on demand also produced a new species of men—the unnecessary fathers.[3] Virtually every fragment of society has bought into this concept, including the church. Inevitably, when we talk about single parents, we mean custodial parents. But noncustodial parents, most often dads, are parents too, and there is virtually no attempt on the part of either the government or church ministry to reach them.

The absence of fathers has created an entire stratum of society that lives in poverty. Although women have many more commercial options than ever before, financial security has been elusive for mother-headed, single-parent households. The vast majority—87 percent—of welfare recipients are in single-parent households. Research indicates that 57 percent of single mothers earn less than fifteen thousand dollars per year.[4] Comparatively, only about 20 percent of single fathers earn below poverty level.[5] It is estimated that 73 percent of the children in single-parent family homes will spend some part of their lives before the age of eighteen in poverty.[6]

Children living in poverty in single-parent households do not suffer simply because they can't afford Nike shoes or the latest CDs. (I actually had one pastor tell me that was the only difference he could see between the children in single-parent families and children from two-parent families in his congregation!) Nor is food the major issue. Most single-parent families do not go to bed starving, although they may be poorly nourished. Food banks are available and are generally used. Single-parent families suffer from a multitude of deficiencies, but not all of them are obvious to the casual observer.

Single-parent families move frequently. At one time, the courts were likely to award the family home to custodial mothers. That is not the case anymore. With the advent of the no-fault divorce, the courts, in community-property states, generally require the family home to be sold and the proceeds split between the two parties. More often than not, the first move to a residence is a temporary solution, necessitating another move in a short amount of time. Even when mothers are awarded the family home, they may not be able to handle all of the costs associated with retaining it, including mortgage, taxes, insurance, repairs, and maintenance. Among the hundreds of single-parent families I have ministered to, I have found that the vast majority of children are caught in a revolving door of changing family households.

The disruption destabilizes the social and educational world of the children. A residential move means the loss of friends, and often pets—elements that normally help ease the pain of family disruption. It may also mean a change in school districts, which, according to David Elkind, is an extremely high stress-producing factor for all children.[7] Due to custody arrangements, children of divorce shuttle back and forth between their parents' homes on weekends, holidays, and summer vacations, sometimes racking up enough miles to give them frequent-flier status. Research indicates that, in their highly mobile life, children of divorce experience profound feelings of isolation, loneliness, sadness, and despair.[8]

I will never forget when my own daughter, at age nine, was forced to leave her friend who lived next door so that her dad could take her to his house. She stood in the middle of the driveway with big tears rolling down her cheeks as she shouted at me, "I am not a Frisbee. You can't just throw me back and forth like you want to. I hate this. You and Dad have a home. When do I get a home?"

Children in single-parent households suffer from lack of opportunity. Their financial situation often prohibits them from participating in athletics, extracurricular activities, camps, and other educational experiences that children from two-parent families can afford. If they have been fortunate enough to receive child support from the absent parent, the support stops being available at the time they most need additional financial assistance to attend college and make the shift from teen to young adulthood. Although many family attorneys urge parents to make provisions for their children's college education, insufficient income or lack of long-term planning often jettison the best of parental intentions.

Finally, financial poverty produces indigence of hope. Mark Fine and Lawrence Kurdek believe their research demonstrates a correlation between the multiple transitions faced by children from single-parent families and those children's lower grade point averages, lower achievement test scores, and a greater likelihood that they will drop out of high school due to, among other things, despair.[9]

Lack of appropriate role models, particularly that of a father, may be one of the leading factors responsible for producing the increasing trend of violence among youth.[10] In our transient society, children of single-parent households rarely have both parents available to them as regular role models. Furthermore, they do not have the benefit of committed grandparents, aunts, uncles, or even long-time neighbors. They may never get to see what a healthy family system looks like. Television sitcoms reflect the society's loss of traditional families. With the notable exceptions of *Cosby* and *The Promised Land*, fathers on television are characterized as irresponsible, loutish, and just plain silly jerks. The more than sixteen million children in single-parent homes see so many household arrangements that resemble their own, that they come to think of them as completely normal.

In the past few years, the number of divorces has leveled off and has even begun to decline. That does not mean, however, that the concept of limited commitment has lost its grip on the American culture. Since 1996, the number of single-parent families due to out-of-wedlock births (40 percent) exceeds the number of single-parent families due to divorce (38 percent). Five percent of single parents have lost their spouse due to death, and 17 percent are in a kind of catch-all category. Their circumstances are varied and include the inability of an individual to effectively parent, due to imprisonment, drug or alcohol abuse, severe physical or mental impairment, etc. (Census Data, 1995).

Most single parents are white because the majority of Americans are Caucasian. However, 25 percent of White households are single-parent led, compared with 65 percent of Black households.[11] Black families have been profoundly changed by the increase in illegitimacy. It is estimated that as many as 80 percent of children born to black mothers in urban areas are born out of wedlock.[12]

Nearly one-third of the unwed mothers are teenagers. The availability of abortion has undoubtedly affected the number of illegitimate births, but how dramatically, we cannot be certain. The vast majority of those are impregnated by men over the age of twenty, making these pregnancies largely cases of statutory rape. As a result, several states have considered new legislation for raising the age of consent for girls from sixteen to eighteen.

Forty years ago, Ingrid Bergman nearly forfeited her career for an adulterous relationship. Today Hollywood stars are increasingly willing to opt for parenthood without the trappings of marriage. Jodie Foster, Madonna, and Michelle Pfeiffer all have shunned the altar but are regularly featured in news magazines as single mothers who have it all. The implicit message to young, unmarried women is that their lives are better because they are not hampered by the presence of a unneeded husband.

The attitude is representative of many college-educated women, commercially successful women. But in an analysis of income patterns in 1994, the median income of a college-educated, single-parent household was significantly lower than the median income of a married-parent, high school–educated household.[13] The reality is that because women tend to have primary custody of the children (which every custodial parent can testify is a full-time job in itself), they have little time or resources to develop better income opportunities.

Childcare is enormously expensive. Even inadequate childcare can eat up more than one-half of the income of parents who earn around one thousand dollars a month. When children become sick, day-care centers may prohibit them from attending. Half-days at school, inclement-weather days, or in-service days all tend to expropriate funds from a single parent's paycheck. Nonpayment of child support is an enormous burden. Less than half of those who are awarded child support receive the money. Approximately 25 percent never receive even the first payment![14]

Women who parent alone are under tremendous financial and emotional pressure. Although they ostensibly have the freedom to be like their Hollywood heroines, the reality—of even a short time of parenting by themselves—is that they come to believe that they cannot manage alone.

Single parents work hard at finding a new mate, often cohabiting prior to their remarriage.[15] It is significant to note that nearly 95 percent of divorced parents ultimately will make a second trip to the altar. Statistics indicate that 70 percent of second marriages involve children.[16] The reasons given for remarriage are typically (1) parents, especially women, need financial help to raise their children; and (2) parents, equally men and women, need parenting help to raise their children.

From the parent's perspective, remarriage solves what appears to be the most difficult of problems. The irony is that children do not do better once their parents remarry. Notions to the contrary, suggesting that remarried families generally provide a more stable environment, tend to be the product of an idealized two-parent-family concept from the 1960s.

In the generation following World War II, the increased accessibility to divorce gave rise to the assumption that single-parent families were "broken" and that broken families could be repaired through remarriage. "Contemporary opinion regarded the single mother household as transitional, and single motherhood itself as a temporary and undesirable status, to be remedied as quickly as possible through marriage or remarriage."[17]

Stepfamilies were portrayed as indistinguishable from intact, two-biological-parent families. *The Brady Bunch*, a television sitcom that featured the remarriage of widowed parents and the bringing together of their combined six children, seemed no different than the sitcom-portrayed biological families of Ozzie and Harriet Nelson and of Ward and June Cleaver. Through the 1970s and 1980s, scholarly opinion continued to support the assumption that two-parent families, in which one adult was a stepparent, were inherently superior to single-parent families.

At a Congressional subcommittee hearing in 1986, historian Tamara Hareven indicated that "divorce today, in a way, reflects a choice people make of replacing a poor marriage by a better marriage—a marriage that works."[18] Although Hareven agreed that divorce may be personally distressful for the children, it gave them an opportunity to escape from a tension-ridden household and gave them a shot at joining a well-functioning stepfamily. As such, divorce and remarriage were seen as a reaffirmation of family life.[19]

That opinion still holds broad-based appeal. Lynn White reported that remarriage by custodial mothers "is likely to produce long-term positive effects for . . . children's experience of family solidarity."[20] Don Swenson emphasizes the contribution that remarried families can make to the variation of family forms, as well as to the strengths of family reality.[21] When University of Southern California sociology professor Constance Ahrons was interviewed by Bob Sipchen of the *Seattle Times,* she talked about the response she received while on a tour publicizing her book *The Good Divorce* (Harper Collins, 1994). Sipchen wrote that

> [P]eople swarmed to say how grateful they were that she was offering ways to make divorce less destructive and showing models that avoided the brutality so often portrayed in the media. They praised her too, she says, for discussing Thanksgiving dinners at which successfully rearranged families break bread with warmth and affection and weddings at which sets of amicably divorced parents walk their daughter down the aisle.[22]

However, Andrew Cherlin and Frank Furstenberg, highly respected sociologists noted for family studies, report on their recent findings and the paradigmatic shift that has resulted:

> Fifteen years ago, the two of us thought that remarriage would improve the overall well-being of children whose parents had divorced. For one thing, when a single mother remarries, her household income usually rises dramatically because men's wages are so much higher, on average, then are women's wages. . . . In addition, the stepparent adds a second adult to the home. He or she can provide support to the custodial parent and reinforce the custodial parent's monitoring and control of the children's behavior. A stepparent also can provide an adult role model for a child of the same gender.

Despite these advantages, many studies now show that the well-being of children in stepfamily households is no better, on average, than the well-being of children in divorced, single-parent households.[23]

Emotional Consequences of Divorce

Emily was a beautiful, sensitive girl. Her creative nature as a child delighted both of her parents. From the very beginning she was quiet and introspective and showed emotional maturity and intelligence far beyond her years. She loved to read and draw and write endless stories. When she was seven, her parents divorced after years of horrible fighting. As soon as her dad left the house, Emily found that she was, most of all, confused. Although she was grateful for the quiet, she couldn't understand why her dad would leave her. As the months went by, she sensed that she had lost control over her life. Tuesday and Thursday nights and alternate weekends were court-ordered to be spent with her father. The rest of the time was spent with her mother. Although her parents had both tried to have everything that she needed at each of their homes, she felt misplaced in both places.

Divorce did little to ease the fighting between her parents. Her father was angry that Emily spent most of her time at his house reading in her room, when he wanted to take her out to have fun. He blamed her mother for Emily's behavior, which he interpreted as rejection.

Her mother was too busy working to have fun, and Emily knew that her mother deeply resented the "Disneyland dad" relationship that her ex-husband had with his daughter. She didn't know how to satisfy both of her parents. It seemed that neither one of them was ever satisfied with her. Eventually her father moved to the other side of the country with a new wife and new stepchildren.

Emily became more and more withdrawn, finding refuge in writing in her journals. She had a few good friends, but she struggled with a sense of inadequacy. Although very attractive, bright, and creative, she saw herself as ugly, fat, and stupid. She felt unable to control any aspect of her life except one. By fifteen, Emily was profoundly bulimic.

In the early 70s, studies began to reflect the emotional effect of divorce upon adults and children. Judith Wallerstein conducted the first longitudinal study of sixty families disrupted by divorce. The results were published in her two books entitled *Surviving the Break-Up: How Children and Parents Cope with Divorces* (Basic Books, Inc., 1980) and *Second Chances: Men, Women, and Children a Decade after Divorce* (Ticknor & Fields, 1989), written with Sandra Blakeslee. In 1982, Archibald Hart, in *Children and Divorce,* chronicled the devastating impact of divorce on children in every age group. In 1986, research from Armand Nicholi entitled "Changes in the American Family" indicated that 90 percent of the children of divorced homes suffered from an acute sense of shock, including profound grieving and irrational fears. Fifty percent of the children in that study reported feeling rejected and abandoned. Most significantly, 37 percent of the children were even more unhappy and dissatisfied five years after the divorce than they had been at eighteen months. In other words, time did not heal their wounds.[24]

The past thirty years of easy divorce have increasingly created a low-commitment culture in which the lives and needs of the children are too often neglected. Parents are unwilling to stay together for the sake of the children and there has developed a casualness in which divorce is used as a stepping stone for personal fulfillment with the expectation that the children will bounce back. The fallout from the divorce process destabilizes the entire family structure, especially the children, who struggle with the lack of control over the chaos in their lives. The consequences for them are evident in these sobering statistics:

- Approximately three out of four teenage suicides occur in households where a parent has been absent.[25]
- Children who grow up in fractured families are less likely to graduate from high school than children from intact families.[26]
- Young daughters of divorce are more likely to be sexually involved, become pregnant more often before marriage, marry younger, and be divorced or separated from their husbands.[27]
- Children from divorced homes, particularly boys, are typically less cooperative and more disruptive, displaying depression, uncommunicative behavior, hyperactivity, aggression, and delinquent behavior.[28, 29]
- Seventy percent of the young men in prison have been reared without a father in the home.[30]

The children of divorce do not have a monopoly on the emotional crisis than ensues when a marriage ends. Barbara Defoe Whitehead has done a remarkable job chronicling the history, attitudes, and consequences of divorce in America in her book *The Divorce Culture*. She assails the attitude of feminists that promoted divorce as valuable for women who have lost their identities in the confines of their marriages.

She defines "expressive divorce" as the one that is self-ishly undertaken to satisfy one's rights, needs, and personal desires with little or no regard for the consequences to the children. Whitehead agrees that divorce sometimes is necessary to escape from dangerous and violent marriages, but she apparently believes that only women engage in expressive divorce. Unfortunately, her harsh and provocative conclusion that reasons other than physical violence constitute "expressive divorce" is unfounded. She has missed some alarming data from one study that indicates that 75 percent of the women sampled indicated a belief that their marriage ended due to "a continuing pattern of abuse."[31] The abuses most often cited were infidelity, verbal/emotional, and physical.

I do not know the intent of Ms. Whitehead, nor do I fully understand her severely judgmental attitude, but I do know that I have yet to meet even one single-parent mother who has divorced for "expressive" purposes. My experience reflects a similar conclusion to the study that finds most women feeling hurt, defeated, betrayed, and humiliated as a result of the divorce and its aftermath.

I spoke recently with a lay counselor in our church about two men he was counseling. Both had affairs that ended their nearly twenty-year marriages. In counseling with these men, they individually acknowledged that they were taken by surprise that their wives were behaving with such hostility toward them. They knew that their marriages were over because of their conduct, but neither could understand why their wives could not just "move on."

"Moving on" requires detachment. Detachment is inconsistent with the disintegration of the one-flesh union. I often liken it to two pieces of paper that have been thoroughly glued together and left over several seasons. When you try to tear them apart, pieces of each one stick to the other. You can't ever be completely free of one another.

Hardly anyone ever talks about the enormous sense of humiliation that pummels the spirit of the innocent party when a marriage ends due to infidelity. It's one thing to know that your mate has violated your marriage bed; it is quite another to know that, because of the divorce, everyone else will know too. Certainly there is the loss of the dream that you would live life, raise your children, and grow old together. There is profound anger as well. But my experience is that the humiliation is the heaviest burden of all. Every micron of self-deprecation that one has ever known bubbles up and whacks you in the head when the betrayal happens. No court can adequately compensate for it.

Thabe's study also indicated that for many of the women who experienced their partner's infidelity, there coexisted a pattern of either emotional or physical abuse. Whitehead acknowledges none of this. Rather, she relates a 1982 survey indicating that as little as one year after their divorce, most women reported that they were happier and had more self-respect than they had during their marriages.[32]

It makes perfect sense that most women would feel better about themselves if they were no longer subject to the type of behavior that destroyed their marriages. The betrayal that manifested itself in either infidelity or abuse is the likely cause of the divorce.

Please understand that I do not encourage divorce. Divorce is beyond horrible. I promote marriage counseling—especially premarital counseling. I am adamant about the need for better communication skills between couples and parents and children. This is a topic the book will more completely discuss in a later chapter. The divorce may ultimately have been unnecessary, but it is unfair to suggest that the woman's intentions were simply selfish or without regard for her children.

At this point, I want to add an anecdotal note concerning the issue of betrayal. Betrayal is generally treated as a psychological issue. Counseling helps in many cases, but often when infidelity and emotional abuse are factors in the divorce, hostility of one or both parties continues far beyond the typical three-year time frame assumed to reflect the adjustment period.

I have found more success in helping single parents "turn around"—with regard to their hostility—when betrayal is treated as a spiritual issue. While disobedience was the act, betrayal was the essence of the original sin. The disobedience betrayed the relationship that Adam and Eve had with God. They were so humiliated that they could not even bear to be seen by God. Adam and Eve betrayed one another: Eve when she coaxed Adam into eating the fruit, Adam when he blamed Eve for eating it. Cain betrayed Abel by killing him. The Second Adam, Jesus, was betrayed by Judas. Et cetera, et cetera, et cetera. Every human life experiences betrayal. Every one of us continues to betray Jesus, even after we accept that He has given His life for us. Betrayal is fundamental to the human condition.

So far, I have talked only about the sense of betrayal felt by women. Men feel betrayed as well. Blankenhorn attests to the notion that since the rise of the women's movement, men are confused about their role in the family and in society. Moving from the center of the family to the periphery has stirred a sense of anger and bewilderment at the diminishment of the father's four traditional roles: (1) irreplaceable caregiver; (2) moral educator; (3) head of family; and (4) family breadwinner.[33] Certainly, many men have been able to make the transition to the "new father" that collaborates with the "new woman," but more often than not, fathers are seen as unnecessary, deadbeat visitors to their own children, sperm donors, or stepfathers. The majority of this transformation has happened since the 1960s!

Blankenhorn convincingly concludes that the exceptionally large number of abusive husbands can find its genesis in the past forty years. Traditionally, the responsibility of being father to a family has socialized men. As that role has diminished or has been seen as increasingly marginalized, men have often responded with the various forms of abuse indicated earlier: infidelity, verbal/emotional, and physical.

My own experience with single fathers who have participated in the single-parent family ministry is that they desire to be real dads. But many simply give up, considering the battle too difficult over the long run. They even have to fight the census bureau, which fails to count fathers when their children are not living with them. The numbers of single parents would be much higher if we were able to see the real picture. Noncustodial fathers are single parents too!

3

CHILDREN IN DANGER

HEN AMY WAS NINE years old, her parents separated. Amy's mother, Joanne, had discovered that her husband, Richard, had been having an affair with his coworker. Although it was the first infidelity that she was aware of, he had always been extremely possessive and controlling. When she discovered the affair she asked him to leave and immediately filed for divorce. Throughout the process, Richard blamed Joanne for seemingly everything that had gone wrong in their marriage. He accused her of being an inadequate wife, telling her that she did not satisfy him sexually. He blamed her for his affair, saying that it was a result of her inadequacy and tried to assure her that the extramarital relationship meant nothing to him. Rather, he said, it was intended to relieve his sexual tensions so that he could actually stay married to her.

At least twice a month, Richard sent Joanne letters that outlined her faults and offered correction for each one, using Scripture verses. He left messages on her answering machine, calling her names and heaping guilt upon her for the damage the divorce was doing to Amy. Periodically, he would call her and tell her that if she would learn how to submit and be a better wife, he would take her back, suggesting that if she did not take him back, she would never be with anyone again because she was unsuitable to be a wife.

Joanne's sense of self crumbled under the onslaught. She began to doubt her own sanity and wondered if Richard was right about her inadequacies. She felt tormented with the suggestions that she would never be in another relationship—that no one else would ever want her. Joanne determined that she would have to prove Richard wrong.

Over a period of two years, Joanne dated nine different men. She would "fall in love" quickly and was certain that each one would result in remarriage. She introduced each one of the men to Amy, assuring her daughter she would soon have a new dad. Amy didn't buy it. As each of the relationships failed, Amy became more cynical and rebellious. Her appearance changed from that of a little girl to that of a young streetwalker. At twelve, her hair was bleached and spiked. She used her money for cigarettes and gothic clothes. Her grades deteriorated until she announced that she was going to drop out of school. Joanne was devastated. What she wanted more than anything was to find a husband so that she could give her daughter a stable home.

Understandably, it is a relatively small number of people who would be interested in acquiring the additional responsibility of long-term commitment to parenting someone else's children. The result is that for a single parent, many dating relationships are short-lived. In addition to feeling the loss of one more adults in their lives, the potential danger to children during this time is disproportionately large. In a study by Leslie Margolin, the analysis showed that 84 percent of nonparental abuse occurred in single-parent households. The preponderance—64 percent—was committed by the mothers' boyfriends.[1]

The burgeoning sexuality of preadolescent and adolescent boys and girls may put them at a distinct disadvantage in attempting to make the adjustment to their new parent's relationships. Hetherington and Clingempeel speculate that adolescents of either gender find it difficult to adjust to a parent's remarriage, because there comes a period in time when these children must come to terms with their own sexuality. To have another adult sexual partner move into the house—especially one for whom the sexual taboo of incest does not exist—may prove to be very disconcerting to the adjustment of all household members.[2] This is certainly true for adolescent girls and their stepfathers. In 1993, it was still legal in thirty-three states for a stepfather to divorce his wife and marry his wife's daughter.

Very little has been said of the amalgamation of adolescent boys and girls from different biological parents into the same household and the opportunity for sexual experimentation or predation that such a situation offers.

The Jacksons were in crisis. When they came to the counselor's office, they were angry, agitated, and blaming one another. Recently, they had learned that Mrs. Jackson's sixteen-year-old son, Jeremy Wright, was sexually involved with Mr. Jackson's fifteen-year-old daughter, Tamara. Jeremy had been living with his father on the other side of the country until two months previous, when they became embroiled in a fight over Jeremy's father's new wife. Jeremy asked to come live with his mother. He had not previously met his mother's new husband, whose wife had died, nor had he met the two children who were suddenly his stepsiblings.

When Tamara's and Jeremy's parents explained to the counselor what had happened, each blamed the other's child for the initiation of the relationship. Mr. Jackson accused Jeremy of being a predator while Mrs. Jackson suggested that Tamara was "on the make." Tamara became defensive over that statement and implied that the overt romantic behavior of Mr. and Mrs. Jackson contributed to the highly energized sexual atmosphere of the household. As far as she was concerned, Tamara did not consider Jeremy her brother. They had met one another only within the past eight weeks and were not related either by blood or by legal status. She enjoyed her relationship with Jeremy and told the adults so.

Mr. Jackson reiterated the predator accusation. Jeremy did not spring to his own defense but basically appeared detached. In follow-up counseling, he admitted that his primary concern was where he would go if he were thrown out of the house. The difficulty with his father could not be resolved, and he did not wish to be sent there. On the other hand, he knew that Mr. Jackson's children did not have anyplace else to go, so Jeremy made an assumption that he would be forced out of the house to be on his own. Although he enjoyed the relationship with Tamara and concurred that it did not feel like a sibling incest to him, either, he appreciated and worried about his vulnerability.

In an effort to separate the two, Mr. Jackson demanded that Jeremy return to his father. However, Mrs. Jackson would not entertain the idea and countered that Tamara should go live with her aunt. Neither would consider any other alternatives.

The situation demonstrates the growing problem of intrafamilial sexual relationships between step-related persons. Although we must differentiate between "real" incest and "technical" incest, the disruption of the household, due to the sexual activity among the offspring, tends to pit one biological unit against the other, effectively eroding the marital bond. Furthermore, because of the greater likelihood of redivorce in previously divorced families, some of these children may see multiple stepparents and stepsiblings.

4

THE REMARRIED FAMILY

LTHOUGH IT MAY OFFEND the vague but oft-cited "family values" of contemporary politicians, therapists, and theologians, the negative depiction of stepfamilies in folk tales may very well be grounded in harsh realities. According to a study by Fine and Kurdek, "Stepparents do not fare well when evaluated alongside biological parents." Ample evidence links children's living in stepfamilies to their behavioral problems.[1]

A brief digression into the origin, symbolism, and metaphor of the term *step* may be appropriate at this point. The word was derived from Old German and Old English terms that were tied to experiences of bereavement and deprivation. *Stoep* was used to convey related designations absent of blood relationships, specifically an orphan. Originally referring only to children, by the sixteenth century the term had been broadened to include replacement parents. The negative connotation that long has been ascribed to replacement parents has fostered a secondary definition of *stepchild*, meaning "a child that fails to receive proper care and attention."[2]

Apparently, these are not merely stereotypical labels for which there is no contemporary credence. A study conducted at the University of Missouri in St. Louis confirms that "children with stepmothers are likely to enjoy less support and endure more conflict than children living with their biological mothers."[3] A similar study indicated that "on statistical measures, relationships in stepfamilies appeared particularly negative between stepfathers and their stepchildren." Furthermore, time did nothing to improve the relationships, which became more and more negative until the marriage ended and/or contact dissipated.[4]

In the earlier-cited study by Fine and Kurdek, the researchers concluded that stepparents cannot merely *think* themselves into being better parents. Rather, the researchers suggest, that the "parenting scripts" of biological parents differ from those of stepparents because "biological ties and shared history" naturally give biological parents— but not stepparents—a "strong investment in their children."[5] Clearly, such circumstances set up an environment of conflict within blended families. According to Robert Emery, "The presence of stepchildren is related to an increased likelihood of divorce in remarriage."[6]

Statistics vary, but the best indicators are that 70 percent to 80 percent of second marriages end in divorce, compared to roughly 50 percent for first marriages.[7] Failure rates climb with each successive marriage. *Education Digest,* February 1995, "Family Patterns Today," reported that "of children whose parents divorce and remarry, half will experience a second disruption (divorce) to family life before reaching sixteen." Cherlin and Furstenberg attest to the "multiple transitions" phenomenon:

> [T]he number of family transitions might impair the adjustment of children in stepfamilies. Having coped with

a divorce, and possibly with the introduction of a live-in partner, these children must now cope with another major change in their family system. . . . [S]tudies have found a relationship between the number of family transitions a child has experienced, on the one hand, and the behavior problems, on the other hand.[8]

Following the arrest of two teens in the gruesome murder of a family of four in Bellevue, Washington, DeeDee Spann reported that as a parole officer she sees the same phenomenon. Ms. Spann indicated that the typical history for repeat offenders includes not only a broken home but also a pattern of successive relationships by the primary-care parent, which results in the "double abandonment"[9] of the children. There seems to be evidence that even fairly good parenting bonds can be broken by redirecting the focus of the parent from the child or children to the quest for (and acquisition of) a new partner. It is that sense of double abandonment that Ms. Spann sees as a common thread among repeat offenders.[10]

No one is suggesting that *all* children who experience "double abandonment" end up as criminals. The concept does suggest, however, that in single-parent households where the parents do not consider parenting their number-one priority, children may be at greatest risk.

Study after study indicates that children do not bounce back from losing a parent the way they bounce back from losing a crayon. But it's not a concept promoted in our culture. In fact the opposite is true. There is a scene in the movie *Clara's Heart* in which Clara, a nanny played by Whoopi Goldberg, tells the single mother that her son is suffering from the neglect of his mother as well as his own personal loss from the divorce. The mother replies, "I must first be healed myself before I can reach out to my son."

"That's not true," Clara tells her simply.

But I can tell you from personal experience that "Take care of yourself first" is what we hear. When I divorced in 1987, I bought all of the books on divorce in the secular and Christian bookstores, and I counseled with my friends. The books, and even my Christian friends, were full of strong advice about my needing to take care of myself before I could take care of my children. Virtually every magazine article and book attributed more resilience to the children than to the adult.

The airline oxygen mask was commonly used as an analogy (i.e., put on your own mask first and then put a mask on your children). I made time for me so that I could "take care of myself." It made sense! All of the magazine covers at the grocery store reinforced my selfish thinking.

My children suffered terribly. The eldest was terrified that I would leave too. For almost a year, I couldn't even go to the bathroom without telling her where I would be. On one occasion, she called 911 and hysterically told them that she was home alone because I had left her. When the police car arrived, they found me on a ladder, putting things away in the garage. I didn't hear my daughter calling for me, and she was too upset to come outside to find me.

Another time, I chased the dog around the corner trying to put a leash on her. My daughter screamed and screamed and screamed as I ran out of her sight. The commotion brought the neighbors running, expecting to find that someone had been ax murdered!

My youngest daughter was so distraught by the constant tension between her parents that she threw up every time her dad took her out to eat. They usually went to Chinese restaurants, so for years, he was convinced she had an allergy to MSG. Only recently she confessed that the thought of having her dad bring her back home and having to listen to his raging about the divorce made her so sick that she inevitably threw up.

Latent responses to divorce among compliant youngsters may encourage parents to believe that their children have weathered the crisis without any consequences. The delayed responses and myths about the resilience of children promote the belief in some parents that the divorce can actually be good for the children. But many studies confirm that children may experience depression, eating disorders, aggressive behavior, and other problems years after the divorce has passed. Adult children of divorce express a lack of trust in their significant relationships, which often results in negative expectations of their ability to have stable families.[11] Children never escape completely unscathed.

The oxygen-mask analogy is inappropriate in terms of parenting as a single person. It assumes an all-or-nothing approach to dealing with the needs of the parent and the children during the time of crisis. Clara was right. It is not true that we are helpless to care for our children until we are completely healed ourselves. It is like putting children in the closet to starve while parents feed hungrily. In many cases, such negligence results in serious physical and emotional abuse.

Scripture poses the same question: "Which of you, if his son asks for bread, will give him a stone? Or if he asks for a fish will give him a snake?" (Matt. 7:9). Parents often need help to realize that they are giving their children stones and snakes while keeping the bread and fish for themselves.

5

SUCCESSFUL
SINGLE-PARENT FAMILIES

YET, THERE IS A PARADOX! In spite of overwhelming obstacles, many single-parent families do succeed. One study indicates that children from committed, single-parent families can, and do, perform as well as children from committed, intact families. The critical element in their success is the evidence of life-skill competency on the part of the primary caregiver, plus the love, support, control, and supervision typically associated with traditional family structure.[1] Unfortunately, it is commonly assumed—by a society that arbitrarily stigmatizes the children in single-parent households—that single-parent families are inherently inadequate to provide those elements. Nancy Morrison quoted, in her study of "Successful Single-Parent Families" from a nationally syndicated news article, that

> Teenagers who had serious delinquency records or mental or emotional health problems were far more likely to

straighten out as adults if they lived in a two-parent family, according to a new study. It's a striking illustration of what we've observed in many instances—the difference a stable family can make to a troubled teenager.[2]

Morrison writes,

The overt message clearly says that two-parent families are preferred. But the implication of the second sentence is even more powerful: a two-parent family is inherently stable while a single-parent family is not![3]

To the contrary, Morrison indicated that most evident in these single mothers was a sense of confidence and pride that they were able to manage being a single parent. Along with this confidence was the development of increased independence, responsibility, and self-esteem in their children.[4]

The study noted, however, that the confidence did not appear full-blown in any of the parents immediately following their divorce. It occurred over a period of time.

[I]n most of the research with single-parent families, the sample has been drawn from families experiencing the first few years of singlehood. According to research (Wallerstein and Kelly, 1980), the average length of time it takes single-parent families to adjust to the divorce is three years. *What is actually being studied is the process of adjusting to the divorce rather than the state of single parenthood.* (Italics mine.)[5]

The length of time needed to adjust, however, is frequently disrupted by the urgent quest for a new partner. As a result, parents do not fully adjust to their single-parent role. Nor do they allow themselves time to experience the confidence that comes when small successes accumulate to surmount the negative effects of the deficit theory and provide an opportunity for parents see themselves and their children as strong, healthy families.

Here is the statement that we do not hear or read enough: A stable family is possible in a single-parent household. Although remarriage can be redemptive, it is not necessary for redemption in the divorce-recovery process. Several recent studies have shown that children do *better* in a committed single-parent household than in blended families. Psychologists are now calling the term "blended families" a misnomer, observing that it is virtually impossible to truly blend them. The household becomes two families living under the same roof.

In light of the significant evidence that children from single-parent households do not do better in blended families but *can do* as well—although they often do not—as children in two-parent households, the objective of ministry to single-parent families is to help the single parent refocus his or her attention on the children so that they can learn to be stable. Being a parent isn't just another lifestyle choice. It is an ethical vocation.

THE THEOLOGY OF
WIDOWS AND ORPHANS

6

ARE THEY REALLY
WIDOWS AND ORPHANS?

I N THE FALL OF 1994, a family in a local church was in crisis. A young mom, with two children under the age of seven, was dying of breast cancer. Her husband had recently finished his internship at a local hospital and had moved on to a residency. John was torn apart by what was happening in his family. The illness of his wife brought the reality of his career choice into an entirely new perspective. He felt like a failure for not being able to help her medically. At the same time, he began to doubt his ability to help others. A desire to spend more time with his ill wife plagued him but the long hours at the hospital left little time for his family when they needed him most. Although the church family rallied around them in their time of need, he could not see past the pain in his life. The week after Thanksgiving, John's wife died.

John said that he almost felt relief at her death. His church family brought him dinners and cleaned his house.

A few of the ladies came by a week after the funeral and put up a Christmas tree and helped John buy some gifts for the kids. They invited the family to events around the holidays. When the season was over, they came by and took down the tree and made plans to supplement his meals for the next six months.

On the other side of town, just before Christmas, another church family was also in crisis. Lynda's husband announced that he was leaving her for another woman. Although Lynda knew that he'd had previous affairs, she was actually surprised by this one. She begged him not to leave until after Christmas, for the sake of the children, but he refused, saying that he had made plans to spend the holidays in Mexico with his girlfriend.

Lynda went to her pastor in tears. He sympathized with her and assured her that God would judge her husband for his infidelity. He heard her pour out her heart over the grief she felt that her marriage was over, and she expressed her stomach-turning fear that she would not be able to manage without him. Although she had a college degree in marketing, she had little work experience because her husband had wanted her to stay home with the children. She was afraid that her husband would resist paying adequate child support, remembering how he had negatively commented on child support when one of his friends divorced. The pastor listened, but he never told another person in the church.

Lynda had been right to worry about child support. Her husband managed to avoid payment for several months. Job hunting for Lynda was tortuous, resulting in only minimum-wage offers. Lynda realized that she could not even pay for day care on the amount she would earn. She chose not to take the jobs and fed her family copious amounts of oatmeal. After the small amount of savings in the bank was gone, she found herself standing in line at the welfare office.

Lynda had stopped coming to church because she was so embarrassed. In February, someone from the congregational care committee called her and asked if she would be willing to provide two meals in the month of April to John's family because his wife had died.

The question that begs asking is "How does the widows-and-orphans theme have any relation to today's single parents?" It's a good question and, frankly, one I encounter over and over as I work, trying to raise awareness of the need for single-parent ministry in churches.

In the case of John, whose wife died, and Lynda, whose husband left her, I submit there ought to have been no difference in how the church related to their needs. Lynda was no more in control of her husband's leaving than John was in control of his wife's cancer. Yet, because of choices made by Lynda's very healthy husband, she was accorded a much lower strata of support by her church. Judgements are commonly made in situations like Lynda's that further damage an already deeply wounded person and drive them away from the body of Christ.

Was Lynda less a widow than John was a widower? Are we called to make those fine distinctions? Would Lynda's circumstances not have qualified her for the "widows" category had she lived in Jerusalem two thousand years ago?

Unfortunately, part of the problem is the number of advancements women have made in the past hundred years. For one thing, women in North America are not held in the same low position that Hebrew women were held in two thousand years ago. There is no longer any question that women have equal intelligence. Today they have the same right to be educated and are actually being educated at a higher rate than men. (One father was overheard telling his daughters that they needed a better education than men, because women are caught in a double bind: women do not earn as much as men for the same work, and women cannot count on men to provide for them anymore.) It is true that women have infinitely more job options than ever before.

Even if we agree that the single parents and their children could be identified as the widows and the orphans of the New Testament, circumstances are so changed that they don't appear to have the same needs. No one would ever think of taking children as slaves to pay off a debt. Women don't have to follow along after the harvesters to pick up the leftover stalks of grain just to eat. Even as little as one hundred fifty years ago, women were still in a very low economic position. But today, especially in light of the women's movement, it is hard to conceive that women who have a college education and children who have $150 running shoes qualify as widows and orphans.

Furthermore, women can and do initiate many of the divorces. Like my church administrator, many Christians feel uncomfortable aiding and giving comfort to people who choose to walk out on their marriages. The irony is that the women's movement, the sexual revolution, and no-fault divorce—all intended to liberate women—have had an increasingly dark side that no one counted on.

When I defined Alison as a widow in need, the church administrator did not agree with me. One of the greatest difficulties I have encountered in church congregations, regarding ministry to single-parent families, has been the use of the word *widow* to define single parents.

Every language has its peculiarities. Some words reflect tremendous preciseness while others do not. We tend to think of New Testament Greek as very exact. And it is. There are four words for the concept of love in Greek. We have only one word. Because of that, we English speakers often do not understand the nuances of Scripture when it talks about love. The way that God loves us (*agape*) is not the way that we love our mate (*eros*) or the way that we love our friends (*filia*). The fourth (*storgé*) defines the affection that we have for our children. Each is quite different; each represents a different emotion, a different level of commitment, and a different response. But in English, each is simply "love."

On the other hand, in the English language, a widow is a woman whose husband has died. We use the word *divorcee* to describe a woman who has been divorced. No longer commonly used, *Maiden, spinster,* and *old maid* have been words used to describe unmarried women of various ages. But the term *widow* in biblical Greek was much more imprecise. The Greek word *chēra* (widow) is derived from the word *chasma,* meaning "a deficiency or a vacancy." A widow was a woman who simply was deficient of a husband. She was a woman whose husband had died, or very likely, a woman whose husband had divorced her. It is conceivable that she could have been a woman who had never been able to marry for a variety of reasons. The issue was not how she managed not to have a husband, but rather the fact that she was deficient of one.

The Hebrew word *almānâh* also means "a desolate place," the prime root word of which is *alâm,* meaning "put to silence" or "unable to speak." These terms make sense when viewed within the cultural context. Women in ancient times had no voice. In both Hellenistic and Roman cultures, women were held in uniformly low position.[1] But in the Hebrew culture, it was lower still. Widowhood was a most-feared fate in the Hebrew tradition. The death of the husband before old age was seen as a retribution for his sins, and it was a retribution in which the widow apparently shared. "The reproach of your widowhood you will remember no more" (Isa. 54:4). In contrast to the other nations of the area, Hebrew law made no provision for the widow (any woman deficient of a husband) except in the case of levirate marriage.[2] In Roman and Greek law, a woman whose husband had died, a woman who had been divorced, or a never-married woman had some rights of inheritance. But in Hebrew legislation, she was passed over entirely.

When I speak of a Hebrew widow as "one whose husband has died," it may appear that I have contradicted myself regarding the use of the term. However, it appears very likely that the idea of widows was expanded to include divorcees.

Divorce was common throughout the Roman Empire in the first century B.C.[3] The precise causes of these divorces have been difficult to assess, but it generally is assumed that because marriage was primarily established for the purpose of producing legitimate offspring, rather than sustaining the individual happiness of the marriage partners, the justification for divorce was often the marriage union's barrenness.[4] However, the early believers knew Jesus' teachings on divorce, and Paul reiterated the insolubility of marriage in his first letter to the Corinthians. Therefore, we might make some assumption that it was not the Christian believers who were divorcing. But it is quite plausible to suggest that women who became believers and were ultimately divorced by their unbelieving husbands—as Paul indicated in the same letter—may very well have been categorized as "widows." This is particularly poignant if the believing woman was divorced with the additional burden of barrenness. Whom would she remarry?

Roman society urged widows to remarry. In fact, a widow between the ages of twenty and fifty was required to remarry within one year or be subject to "considerable material disadvantage."[5] With no rights of inheritance, no male advocate (a son, brother, or father would do), and no husband, a woman, whether her culture was Roman, Hellenist, or Hebrew, had few job options. Most commonly, she would become a prostitute.

The only free individuals more vulnerable than widows were their children. Across the Sea of Galilee, children were said to have been regularly sacrificed to the pagan gods in the region of the Gerasenes where Jesus sent a legion of demons into a herd of pigs (Luke 8:26–38). Actually, children were generally welcomed into marriages—indeed it is widely held that the only purpose of marriage was to produce children. Criminal charges likely would have been leveled at any woman who attempted to abort her child or to abandon it. The exception occurred in cases of desperate poverty. Desperate poverty was widespread and was particularly the case for widows.

The practice of putting a child out, or "exposure" as it was called, was apparently anything but uncommon. There were no government-supported orphanages or adoption agencies. Most communities had well-known places where unwanted children were left. Justinian reported that the church in Thessalonica was such a place.[6]

It wasn't until sometime between A.D. 320 and 355 that Constantine issued sanctions against parents who sold or pledged their children in payment of debt. Until A.D. 529, it was common practice for children found abandoned to be taken into households to be reared as slaves. Justinian, horrified at the mercenary motives of the finders, forbade the practice and ordered that children rescued from exposure were to be raised as free children.[7]

7

BIBLICAL HISTORY OF SINGLE-PARENT AND BLENDED FAMILIES

T HE BIBLE VIVIDLY ILLUSTRATES the complex variations of families in a fallen world. It took but six generations for the descendants of Adam to fall into polygamy. In spite of God's admonishment in Genesis 2:24 concerning monogamy, Lamech, from the independent and prideful line of Cain, took two wives in an apparent attempt to multiply his blessings. Lamech's wives produced several children, including Noah.

Although there is no record of dissension between the wives and among the children of Lamech, discord is obvious in the story of Abraham, Sarah and Isaac, and Hagar and Ishmael. After Sarah's death, we are told that Abraham married Keturah, who bore him at least six more sons. Before he died, he gave some gifts to the children of his concubines as well as to his other children, but sensing the likely outcome of his decision to leave all that he owned to Isaac, he sent his other children away so that they might not trouble his firstborn, legitimate son.

The range of family problems is even more conspicuous in the story of Jacob and his two wives, Rachel and Leah. It was specifically the hatred and jealousy for stepchildren and half-siblings that resulted in the brutal attack upon Joseph. Moses testified that even before he heard God's voice, he was drawn to his biological family over his adopted family, in spite of the fact that identification with the first led to poverty and exile, while remaining with the second would have been replete with power and wealth.

Hannah, the mother of Samuel, was provoked and disparaged by Peninnah, the other wife of Hannah's husband Elkanah. David's household was full of all types of family dysfunction, including rape, incest, jealousy, and murder. The interference of Bathsheba, the favored wife of David and mother of Solomon, ignited the fury of Adonijah as he attempted to ascend to the throne of David near to the time of his father's death. In a conspiracy that pitted half-brothers against one another, resulting in the death of one, we see the astounding convolution of hatred and jealousies that arise in families where blood lines are aparently not the ties that bind.

Some would suggest that the Old Testament reveals an extended-family model for the care and nurture of children. However, the adversities of the Old Testament families, which included multiple wives and a collection of half-siblings, indicate that God's best may not have been represented in that model. Rather, God intended for marriage to result in a one-flesh union—a monogamous relationship that symbolized His covenant with mankind. Children would be added to the union, in part to symbolize His blessing and His continued renewal of the covenant. It was that model God called "good."

There is nothing in Scripture to suggest that blended families were able to function better in the time of Sarah and Abraham than they are today. The types of families illustrated in the Old Testament are not evidence of what families should be, but rather, they are evidence of what happens to families when they do not subscribe to God's ideal.

On the other hand, we do see the extraordinary care and compassion God has for the widow with children. As soon as she knew that she was pregnant, Hagar began to hate Sarah, and her feelings were reciprocated for the entire thirteen years they lived with Abraham.

> "And [Sarah] said to Abraham, 'Get rid of that slave woman and her son, for that slave woman's son will never share in the inheritance with my son Isaac.'" (Gen. 21:10)

But contrast the exile into which Sarah sent Hagar with the compassion and grace God had for Hagar and Ishmael.

> "God heard the boy crying, and the angel of God called to Hagar from heaven and said to her, 'What is the matter, Hagar? Do not be afraid; God has heard the boy crying as he lies there. Lift the boy up and take him by the hand, for I will make him into a great nation.'" (21:17b–18)

Consider also an event in the life of Elijah:

> The prophet Elijah encountered the widow at Zarephath that God chose to provide him with food and water. She used all that she had. For her faith and obedience, the small amount of flour and oil continued to be replenished day after day until the drought lifted. When the widow's son died of an illness, the prophet Elijah lay on top of him and begged for God for his life: God

breathed life back into the son of the widow through the prophet. Trusting that God would be her provision, the widow and her child were fed and protected. (1 Kings 17:13–24)

Elisha had an encounter with a different widow:

The wife of a man from the company cried out to Elisha, "Your servant my husband is dead, and you know that he revered the Lord. But now his creditor is coming to take my two boys as his slaves."[1]

As a mother, I can only imagine the terror in that woman's heart. After losing her husband, she seemed destined to lose her sons to the man who loaned them money. What would happen to her? The woman was very poor. Without a husband, without sons to take care of her, she probably would have died of starvation one day along the side of the road.

God became her provider and protector. In this case, just so that we can be sure that it is God, the husband to the widow and the father to the fatherless, and not the prophet, the woman was sent into her home with her sons only. Alone they collected jars and alone they sold the abundance of oil that allowed the widow to repay the family's debts and keep her sons free. Elisha neither went with her into her home nor suggested that anyone else was necessary for her to save her children. God alone provided all that was needed.

The New Testament is also peppered with stories of widows. During the ministry of Jesus, the circle of ministry opened wider to include others who may not have been thought of as needy or in the widows-and-orphans category.

One of my favorite accounts is of the Samaritan woman at the well, recorded in John 4. You may never have thought of her in the way I will present her. She is something of a mystery. Her circumstances may reveal more about her in the light of some different questions.

This unnamed woman lived in Samaria, a region that lay between Judea in the south and Galilee in the north. The area stretched from the Mediterranean Sea on the west to the Jordan River on the east. Most of the time, Jews avoided going through Samaria by crossing the Jordan while they were still in Judea and traveling up the eastern bank until they could cross back over into Galilee. Choosing this route testified that Jews would go miles out of their way to avoid mixing with Samaritans.

When Jesus sent out his twelve disciples, He specifically told them to avoid Samaria: "Do not go among the Gentiles or enter any town of the Samaritans" (Matt. 10:5). Yet, just a little while later, when Jesus was with John the Baptist and the number of baptisms were beginning to arouse the suspicions of the authorities, Jesus left to return to Galilee. John says, "Now he had to go through Samaria" (4:4). He didn't *have* to go through Samaria because of geography, he *had* to go through Samaria because of His mission. And His mission was to one person.

In a little village named Sychar—at around noon when it was so hot that a drop of water would have sizzled on the stones at the well—Jesus sat down to rest, sending His disciples on ahead to buy food. Jesus did not have anything with which to draw water for a drink, so He waited. The woman who came along, Scripture tells us, had been married five times and was living with yet another man. Her shame must have been great, for she ventured out into the heat of the day rather than at a time in the early evening when the other women went to draw their water.

When Jesus asked her for a drink. She undoubtedly was suspicious, for there was tremendous hostility between the Jews and Samaritans. Jews considered Samaritans unclean. The woman implied that Jesus would have to drink from an unclean cup. Then Jesus said something of a riddle: "If you knew the gift of God and who it is that asks for a drink, you would have asked him and he would have given you living water" (John 4:10).

I can imagine the woman saying to herself, *Yeah, right. This well is 138 feet deep. You don't have anything to draw with, and you're telling me that you can give me living water?* She didn't understand that Jesus wanted her to focus on water and not the bucket.

Jesus brought up the business about her husbands she was undoubtedly caught off guard. But she must have been very quick witted for her response was immediate: "You are a prophet." Attempting to rescue herself from a sticky situation, she affirmed that both Jews and Samaritans worshiped the same God. The Samaritans worshiped on the mountain, the Jews claimed that worship must be in the temple in Jerusalem. Jesus compassionately told her that the Messiah would come from the Jews, but that the time was coming, in fact already had arrived, that true worshipers would worship the Father in spirit wherever they were.

Can you imagine her shock when, after saying that, yes, she knew the Messiah was coming, Jesus—still thirsty and sitting in the hot noonday sun—told her that He was the Messiah?

This wonderful narrative from John illustrates the depth of Jesus' love for all people. His mission was about transformation. He expressed no condemnation for the woman's marital history—only the awareness that He knew. Why? Why bring it up?

Commentaries suggest that it was to point out that no sin is unforgivable in Jesus' eyes. True, but then why not simply say that she was a woman of immoral character. What is the issue of multiple marriages?

In our culture, marrying five times has definite implications of lack of commitment, if not loose morals. At the time that Jesus was sitting by that well, the law did not allow for women to initiate divorce. Men were able to divorce their wives for any minor grievance. Although the Samaritans were not bound by Hebrew law, they did have the Pentateuch as their Bible. They likely had similar regulations.

Women were little more than chattel. Those who had been turned out of their marriages had virtually no opportunity apart from another marriage to survive, save prostitution. If she were barren, she may not have been able to marry a second or third time, since marriage was generally for procreative purposes. If she were not barren, could she have had children who remained in their fathers' households? Could this woman have been a single mother? Could she have been a woman who chose to marry multiple times rather than consider prostitution?

At this point, only Jesus knows for sure. He didn't condemn her. Rather, He had compassion on her. He did not make the distinction that she was not in need because her husband had not died. For her obedience, He became her provider of living water and her protector from the townsfolk. He transformed her from a vulnerable woman into a disciple of the Gospel, although her outward circumstances had not changed.

God tells us that He will be a husband to the widow and a father to the fatherless. I don't believe that it is important to him how it is that they are no longer married.

Single parents do not surprise God. Neither is He is offended by them. God loves them and has a plan for them. What has transpired in their lives may not have been His best for them, but He knew it would happen from the beginning of time. In His omniscience and love, God can give single parents everything they need to be the best single parents they can be.

Jesus died for the widow, for the divorced, and for the unwed parent. He commits that He will never leave them nor forsake them, nor give them more than they can handle. God is deadly serious concerning the care of the widow and the orphan. He warned the Israelites,

> Do not take advantage of a widow or an orphan. If you do and they cry out to me, I will certainly hear their cry. My anger will be aroused and I will kill you with the sword; your wives will become widows and your children fatherless. (Exod. 22:22–24)

God is just as serious about single parents today. Like the woman at the well, He wants to transform them from hurting and needy individuals into joyous bearers of the Gospel. So far, the church is acting like the disciples, who didn't even want to go through Samaria. Have you ever considered that perhaps because we do not take care of the widow and the orphan, they are on the increase for that reason?

8

THE CHURCH AND THE SINGLE PARENT

J EANIE WAS A SINGLE PARENT in her early thirties. Her parents had been actively involved in church from a time long before her birth. She gave her life to Jesus as a young child and grew up to go to a small Christian college in Minnesota, her home state. Jeanie met her husband Jake there. In her junior year, she dropped out of school to marry him. Together they had two children and continued to be active in a local church after their move to the Portland area.

Jeanie lived by her belief that her husband was absolute head of the household. So after eleven years of marriage, when he asked her for a divorce, she was in total shock. She claimed that she never saw it coming. She overlooked signals that things were not well, choosing only to be supportive while Jake worked eighty hours a week at starting a new company.

Jake explained to her that he had found someone in his office who worked alongside him, helping him with the building of the business and with getting through the roller-coaster emotions associated with it. This woman was very intelligent, fun-loving, and spontaneous. Jake claimed that she stimulated his thinking and dreaming in a way he had never experienced in a woman before. He told Jeanie that it was not that he didn't care for her, he just found her very dull and uninterested in his life. He could not imagine spending the next forty years enduring the boring monotony of the past eleven.

After seeing her pastor, Jeanie agreed the divorce was biblically possible on the basis that her husband had been unfaithful to her. Jake was generous with child support, allowing Jeanie to continue to stay at home with the children, at least until the youngest was in high school. Although she felt like a failure, she never let the sadness show on her face. People in the church were amazed at how well she handled the situation.

Jeanie's demeanor after the divorce elicited feelings of sympathy and cautious optimism among her friends. Off-handedly they asked her when she was going to start dating again, and occasionally, they actively encouraged her to remarry for the sake of her children. She carefully considered their advice and reasoned that maybe God was telling her to remarry through the words of her Christian friends. She could see the merits of their advice. God Himself instituted the two-parent family. Being a single parent seemed ungodly somehow. The programs she listened to on Christian radio emphasized the importance of having two parents in the household. They also discussed how children in single-parent families almost always end up in trouble. It frightened her. She did not want her children to experience the negative effects of a broken home.

As she looked around her in church one Sunday, she observed that she didn't see any other families that didn't have two parents. Looking at her bulletin, she saw a drawing of the church with a young mother and father holding the hands of their two children and walking into the building. It made her feel inadequate. Even though she loved her church, she concluded that she and her children would probably stand out like a sore thumb. In her heart, she knew that if she didn't remarry, it would be hard to feel comfortable there over a long period of time.

When Jeanie's friends arranged for her to meet a single man in the church, she saw it as God opening the doors for her to make her family whole again.

Is the church a safe place for single-parent families? If it is, single parents rarely sense it. Research indicates that only 5 percent of single-parent families—compared with 35 percent of two-parent families—regularly attend church. What is it in the character of the church that discourages single parents from attending?

Apart from those denominations that consider remarriage following divorce to be biblically illegal, the traditional view in the church has been to consider remarriage to be the best solution for the problems associated with the single-parent family. Since the Reformation, the Protestant church has promoted marriage over singleness. To some degree, it was a reaction to the monasticism espoused by the Roman Catholic Church. However, it was also a response to the widely held belief that sexual desires, particularly in women, raged out of control and that marriage was the appropriate solution to wantonness.

If that kind of reasoning sounds ridiculous and not relevant in these years close to the second millennium, I challenge you to ask any single mother if she has ever felt put off by another woman in the church who has behaved as though she was "after" her husband. In my many years of ministry, this is a commonly voiced complaint by single parents. One woman related the following incident to me:

"When I introduced myself to a friendly-looking couple at the back of the church, the woman asked me if my husband was with me. I said, 'No, I am divorced.' The woman physically backed up and put her arm around her husband's. 'Oh,' she said in a syrupy voice, 'I'm sorry.' Then she kind of giggled and said, 'But you can't have mine.' Then to her husband she cooed, 'You belong to me. Right, honey?'

"I mean, she might as well have crossed her fingers in an X in front of my face or thrown garlic at me or pounded a wood stake in my heart. I don't know—whatever they do to keep the vampires away. I was so embarrassed. I hadn't done anything except introduce myself. I could never go back there. The last thing in the world I am looking for now is another husband. It was so insulting! She made me feel so cheap."

"Cheap" is one of the many labels that single parents wear. In classes with single parents, I often ask them to list some of the labels they sense coming from the church community. Always mentioned are "failure," "husband-grabber," "incompetent," and "sinful."

I don't believe that churches intentionally project these labels. Sometimes the situations are as subtle as Jeanie feeling uncomfortable with the drawing on the front cover of the bulletin. Other times, they are as overt as the story I just related.

Neil Clark Warren argues that marriage within the Protestant church has been raised to a position of near idolatry.[1] As I have observed numerous pastors in churches who marry people for the second time, I am convinced that they have fallen prey to notions of romanticism. One pastor even shared with me that he could never consider telling a couple that remarriage might not be a good idea, even if he believed it was not, because he could not bear to upset their wedding plans!

In the mid-70s, singles ministries developed out of the need of singles to be seen as whole people for whom God had a purpose. Twenty years later, single people still struggle to feel integrated into the larger congregation. Lots of single parents find a place for themselves in singles groups, but often at the expense of caring for their own children. Single parents with the responsibilities of children have (or should have) a very different agenda for their lives than people who have never married and have no offspring. Childcare, school, homework, bedtime, etc., are all considerations that parents—whether married or single—have for their families. But singles groups are generally very social and typically are geared for "adults only." Not only do they exclude children when the children of single parents desperately need their parents' attention, but they also provide sometimes-insurmountable temptations for single parents to put activities that will lead to recoupling ahead of the needs of their children. In terms of characteristics, single-parent families are closer to married couples than they are to singles, but their singleness precludes them from inclusion in many family ministries.

Family has taken on a very narrow meaning. The term broken family, referring specifically to families of divorce, indicates a lack of wholeness. The implication is that only families with two parents are whole. Single-parent households, by that definition, are inadequate. Even to be called a family, children with one parent are attributed a different status—a hyphenated qualifier. Clearly the perception is that they are not the same!

Dr. Dennis Guernsey contended that family is a verb, not a noun.

> Biblically speaking, the concept of family has to do with being the family of God, the people of God. I've come to believe that the concept of family is less a noun and more a verb when we're talking about who we are as the people of God. By that I mean, family is what we do for one another rather than some sort of descriptor of who we are in relation to one another.
>
> I'm convinced now that we are guilty of arguing more for a Victorian ideal of the family than a biblical ideal. The Victorian ideal was probably true for a period of time in human history beginning with the late 1800s—but even then it was only true for the upper and upper middle class. This ideal then spilled over into the middle class of America. . . . Unfortunately, today's church is trying to make the Victorian version of family a biblical version. But it just ain't so.[2]

Many times throughout history, the church has had large numbers of single parents and children. Often after wars, when the widows looked like "real" widows because their husbands had died, ministry from the church was not as reticent as it is today. The labels that single parents feel suggest an assumption, on the part of others, of sexual sin. That perception of sin tends to isolate single parents, especially single mothers, who are so obvious and so visible. Single fathers may escape the stigmatization—probably because they remarry sooner and are less likely to have custody of their children. As a result, they do not "stand out" in the way single mothers do.

Biblically, we know God's intention for families. God says, "I hate divorce" (Mal. 2:16). Neither is procreation outside of a marriage what God had in mind for families. God's *best* is for two biological parents to rear their own children, produced by the one-flesh union. A natural order of priorities is established—God first, then spouse, then children. Although the marriage (or the union that produced the child, irrespective of the legal component) has been broken, what is it that suggests that we can casually reorder God's ordained priorities and insert another unrelated person into the schedule?

Theologically, it may be a matter of stewardship. For every person who has produced a child, the priority of physical and spiritual well-being of that child is well documented in Scripture. Consider Matthew 18:6: "But if anyone causes one of these little ones who believe in me to sin, it would be better for him to have a large millstone hung around his neck and to be drowned in the depths of the sea." But there is also a case to be made of stewardship over ourselves.

I said it before, but I'll say it again. Divorce is a spiritual paradox. While it represents the failure of a relationship that was intended to survive, once broken, it represents the opportunity for spiritual growth and renewal of obedience to God's will. It is extremely problematic to interrupt the process God has allowed—the process of bringing individuals closer to Him in their need—by concluding that marriage is the best solution. Remarriage may in some cases be biblically legal, but it may not be wise.

Congregations have good reason to be troubled by the increase of single-parent family households. The rise of households headed by only one parent testifies to a breakdown in the values and morals in our society. But the community of believers should be even more troubled that single-parent families are not in church where they can be "familied"—where they can experience the love of Christ through His people, who can model values and morals.

Most pastors lack a personal understanding of divorce. They are inexperienced in dealing with the struggles associated with parenting alone or with blending families. They may not have had the opportunity even to think through the issues of single parenting, remarriage, and blended families. As a result, they may confuse the intention God has for children to be reared by two biological parents with the implicit assumption that a single parent is inherently inadequate. A second, more errant assumption is that step-parents are an adequate alternative to biological parents.

The consequence is a not-so-subtle pressure that advocates remarriage and the blending of families over single parenting. Unfortunately, as we have seen, there is significant conflict between this philosophical perspective and the empirical evidence. Remarriage motivated by an idealized concept of family and the need for parenting help or economic assistance compromises God's intent for His people.

Divorce is deplorable, but it must be treated with the empathy and mercy that people need when facing one of the most traumatic times in their lives. Likewise, the rise in illegitimate births has created an unresolved tension for Christians who object to abortion but who see welfare mothers as a scourge on society. Even though the church may encourage adoption, few church communities have a venue through which to care for unwed mothers. The sad fact is that it is easier for a woman who has chosen an abortion to receive ministry in the church than it is for a woman who has chosen to keep her child and appear as an unwed mother.

9

THE HIDDEN
MISSION FIELD

A CLOSE FRIEND OF MINE sits on the mission board in his church. His passion for people who have not had the opportunity to know Jesus Christ is intoxicating. Sometimes his arms sweep in a gigantic, 180-degree gesture as he speaks about areas of the world where there are too few missionaries to do the work. "Think of all of the millions of people who are unsaved in that part of the world," he has said to me. "It is so obvious that we need to send more missionaries there."

Certain mission fields in the world are obvious. I am grateful that people like my friend have been called to respond to the need for the Gospel in places such as the former Soviet Union, Africa, Southeast Asia, and Central America.

There is a huge mission field right here. I am stunned that it continues to be overlooked. Single-parent families in the United States represent a mission field as large as the entire population of Central America.[1] The overwhelming majority of them do not attend church. Some of them are born-again believers who simply do not feel welcome. But they are not obvious. Rather, they represent a hidden mission field camouflaged by the society around them that looks just like us. We've missed them and they are right under our noses!

Morals, values, love, community, and compassion are not being imparted to these families through the church. Whatever values, morals, and community they get come from somewhere else. And the somewhere else has been responsible for the continuing escalation of the numbers of single-parent families in the United States. Over the past ten years, membership in churches has declined 9.5 percent while the population has increased 11.4 percent. It is estimated that 2.7 million church members fall into inactivity every year.[2] We don't know how many of those are single parents, but if we were to reverse the process—that is, increase the church attendance of the single-parent families in their communities—it is likely that over a period of time, the number of single-parent families would go down.

Consider how the church exploded in the first century. Widows and orphans were an important component of the first-century churches. Paul expressed in his letters to Timothy how the early church was to respond to the huge numbers of widows and orphans. He admonished the church to care for them in an intentional way.

John Chrysostom wrote that the church in Antioch cared for three thousand widows.[3] Josephus reportedly wrote to Rome that the citizens were astounded that these people calling themselves Christians cared not only for their own widows, but for others as well. Cornelius, a bishop in Rome during the late second century, reported that the Roman church was supporting no less than fifteen hundred widows.[4]

When we talk about revival in the church, we must consider that the single-parent families are ripe for harvest. The church will explode if we intentionally minister to these families. It exploded in the first century when those churches ministered to widows and orphans. Unfortunately, my observation is that most churches are not even considering single-parent families as viable outreach targets. And what may even be less palatable is the notion that many churches may consider single-parent families as an outreach target that they do not want.

The Biblical Mandate

As we read Scripture, there are multiple references to the widow and the orphan. God sees Himself as their guardian.

> He defends the cause of the fatherless and the widow, and loves the alien, giving him food and clothing. And you are to love those who are aliens, for you yourselves were aliens in Egypt. (Deut. 10:18–19)

The widow, the orphan, and the alien represent the most vulnerable in God's economy. They are His, and they are not to be abused or neglected.

> When you are harvesting in your field and you overlook a sheaf, do not go back and get it. Leave it for the alien, the fatherless, and the widow, so that the Lord your God may bless you in all the work of your hands. When you beat the olives from your trees, do not go over the branches a second time. Leave what remains for the alien, the fatherless, and the widow. When you harvest the grapes in your vineyard, do not go over the vines again. Leave what remains for the alien, the fatherless, and the widow.

Remember that you were slaves in Egypt. That is why I command you to do this. (Deut. 24:19–22)

Both times God reminds Israel, "You were vulnerable, you were abused. I took care of you, and now you must remember to take care of those less fortunate." The New Testament repeats the concept:

With the measure you use, it will be measured to you— and even more. (Mark 4:24)

Give, and it will be given to you. A good measure, pressed down, shaken together and running over, will be poured into your lap. For with the measure you use, it will be measured to you. (Luke 6:38)

In the Old Testament, God used a specific formula, just to make sure the thick-headed among His people knew what to do. Don't pick up the leftover sheaf, don't beat the branch or go over the vine a second time.

That's not all. God goes on to say even more about His intent for the widow, the orphan, and the alien:

When you have finished setting aside a tenth of all your produce in the third year, the year of the tithe, you shall give it to the Levite, the alien, the fatherless, and the widow, so that they may eat in your towns and be satisfied. (Deut. 26:12)

The objective is not like the other two verses, from which one might get the idea that the widows, orphans, and aliens get the leftovers that may or may not be enough. Beyond what they are able to glean, the widow, orphan, and alien are to be given a tenth of the tithe, that they may be *satisfied*. Why? It goes back to the issue of their inability to care for themselves. They are vulnerable because they have no legal status, no one to advocate for them except God, no options beyond what God provides for them through His people.

God is serious about His command:

> Do not take advantage of a widow or an orphan. If you do and they cry out to me, I will certainly hear their cry. My anger will be aroused, and I will kill you with the sword; your wives will become widows and your children fatherless. (Exod. 22:22–24)

The harshness of the Old Testament is not softened by Jesus as he characterizes the separation of the sheep and the goats:

> "Depart from me you who are cursed, into the eternal fire prepared for the devil and his angels. For I was hungry and you gave me nothing to eat, I was thirsty and you gave me nothing to drink, I was a stranger and you did not invite me in, I needed clothes and you did not clothe me, I was sick and in prison and you did not look after me." They also will answer, "Lord, when did we see you hungry or thirsty or a stranger or needing clothes or sick or in prison and did not help you?" He will reply, "I tell you the truth, whatever you did not do for one of the least of these, you did not do for me." (Matt. 25:41–45)

Jesus lives in us. He *is* the widow, the orphan, and the alien. When James tells us, "Religion that God our Father accepts as pure and faultless is this: to look after orphans and widows in their distress and to keep oneself from being polluted by the world," (1:27) he is speaking with the consistent admonition that we are to take care of those less fortunate than ourselves—those who are vulnerable in our midst. The widow and the orphan are in our midst. The alien and the stranger refer to those who live outside our community or those who come from outside our community. But there is no doubt that the first order of business is to care for those within our own communities.

It is *pure* religion, James said, implying that having a religion that does not take care of the widow and the orphan is phony baloney.

> Woe to you scribes and Pharisees, hypocrites, because you devour widows' houses, even while for a pretense you make long prayers; therefore you shall receive greater condemnation. (Matt. 23:14 NASB)

> Jesus said, "Love the Lord your God with all your heart and with all you soul and with all your mind. This is the first and greatest commandment. And the second is like it. Love your neighbor as yourself." (Matt. 22:37–39)

Our neighbor is in our midst, and the most vulnerable in our midst are the widow and the orphan. Eighty-seven percent of welfare recipients are in single-parent family households!

God has gifted me with a strong sense of image with His word. In returning home from a single-parent family conference, I was praying about the imagery that I should use to convey how important this ministry is. God showed me a thermometer. Caring for the widow and the orphan is like a thermometer that measures how much we love Him. It is true that many churches send missionaries (or more likely, money for missionaries) around the world. But in our own communities, the thermometer—the one that shows how much we love God by caring for the widow and the orphan—is covered in layers of frost. There is no line rising out of the mercury ball.

Single-parent family ministry within the body of Christ is so new that we are just beginning to develop resources. Despite the fact that literally one-third of the families with children under the age of eighteen are single-parent families, there are only four full-time pastors to this population in the United States today![5]

> The harvest is plentiful, but the workers are few. Ask the Lord of the harvest, therefore, to send out workers into his harvest field. (Matt. 9:37–38)

MINISTRY TO
WIDOWS AND ORPHANS

10
WHERE DO WE
GO FROM HERE?

T HE PURPOSE OF THIS BOOK is to raise the awareness of the need. Theologically, it is a mandate. Socially, it is a must. Then it is up to you in your church, in your community, to begin to develop a ministry to this hidden mission field. The remainder of this book is dedicated to helping churches—large and small—work through the issues in a systematic fashion. There are little pockets of ministry happening in a few churches around the country. From them, and from years of doing single-parent family ministry myself, I have gleaned some wisdom to pass on to you. The start up of any new ministry is not easy, but I know that if God calls you, He has already, in some ways, equipped you. Pray. That's the first thing to do.

Let me say that again. Prayer is the foundation of your single-parent family ministry. I know in my heart that God is beginning to raise up an army to go out into this mission field. I see it when I go around the country to teach seminars and workshops. I see it in the spirits and on the faces of men and women who are being called. I believe in my head and in my spirit that this ministry must be embraced by every community in the nation before we will see a revival sweep through the land. Only then will we see a renewal of the morals and values that have fallen into decay among the people.

So pray! *Spend a season in prayer*. Pray for God to make clear your call. Pray that God will begin to soften the hearts of the members of your congregation. Pray that He will bring others around you that have a heart for this ministry as well. Pray for the team that He will build. Pray for wisdom. Ask others to pray with you and for you and your team.

After your ministry is off the ground, don't forget to pray even more. Satan will want to destroy a ministry that will be as effective as an SPFM (single-parent family ministry) can be. You can count on that. I try to have a variety of prayer teams, each praying for specific aspects of the ministry as well as specific single-parent families. We have postcard-size forms that single parents can fill out, indicating their prayer requests. The forms are given to the prayer teams to make sure that every aspect of the ministry is covered.

I ask the single parents to pray for one another as well. For many, it is the first time that they have attempted to pray. Without a lot of hoopla, we encourage single parents to pray for their children. Later, we are able to share answers to prayer in class. What a wonderful testimony God allows for these precious single parents to share with one another.

Single-Parent Family Ministry Is a Needs-Driven Ministry

A comprehensive single-parent family ministry has multiple components: spiritual; emotional, for both children and adults; physical—that is, practical; and social, for both children and adults. An effective ministry integrates all of them to some degree. Let's break them down so we can see what we are dealing with.

Spiritual. One of the reasons single-parent family ministries need to be in the church, as opposed to being provided by secular-community programming, is the desperate lack of spiritual understanding in our culture. Only through the church do you have the opportunity to offer the Gospel unfettered to this hidden mission field.

Children and single parents alike need discipleship. They need to know that God loves them and will care for them. The healing of their pain is never complete without the salvation of Jesus Christ.

Emotional. The emotional pain is real and needs to be addressed. However that is done, either in classes or in one-on-one ministry, the importance of support groups and counseling cannot be overstressed. The same is true for both parents and children. Unfortunately, most single parents take their own emotional needs seriously but tend to neglect the emotional needs of their children. Often the children are unable to verbalize their needs, so they may go unnoticed. An effective program will allow the children to express their feelings and will promote in them a sense of being valued.

Physical. This is largely a financial issue. Actually, it's the lack of finances to provide necessities, such as childcare, food, clothing, housing, and an automobile. Indeed, some single parents don't have financial problems. However, we have already seen how many single parents live below the poverty level. It is critical for every SPFM to understand that meeting these needs is a fundamental part of the ministry. Parents cannot focus on emotional healing or spiritual growth when they cannot feed their children or pay the rent.

Life skills. Many single parents are in difficulty because they lack the life skills that others of us take for granted. In a society that has become increasingly transient, extended families are not available to coach young parents, to mentor children, or even to offer friendly advice as things are going astray. Learning new life skills will make the difference between single-parent families continuing the same faulty behavior that contributed to their situation and having the ability to move forward and make good decisions in the future. Life skills that I observe are most lacking are

- New job skills or retraining
- Budget- and money-management training
- Parenting skills, including discipline training
- Communication—talking and listening skills that produce conflict resolution skills.

Social. Single-parent families feel isolated. For many single-parent families, there is no family nearby nor any strong social support. Friends during the marriage tend to fall away after the marriage ends. Many families are not supportive of a never-married, single mother. Social opportunities with other families are always appreciated. There can be times when just adults get together, but there should be ample opportunities for whole families to play together as well. Children need to see other single-parent families as well as two-parent families that function.

God built us to be in fellowship. My experience has taught me that it is necessary for at least one-quarter of the ministry to have some social aspect to it. That is not a hard-and-fast rule but rather a flexible guide to the development of the SPFM.

11

CHURCH
LEADERSHIP ISSUES

YOU WILL NEED TO BUILD a leadership team for your SPFM.
How you do that will depend, to a great degree, on
the governance of your church. In choosing a leadership team, pay close attention to the characteristics of
the players. It is a servant-leader that you are looking for:
But let the greatest among you become as the youngest and
the leader as the servant" (Luke 22:26).

Leadership is a gift. It is an art. In the body of Christ, it is
a mission that God has laid upon someone for a particular
purpose. Think about what a leader chosen by God does. A
leader glorifies God by exercising his or her own giftedness
through the power of the Holy Spirit. A leader is wise, humble,
courageous, self-disciplined, discerning, patient, and authen-
tic. A leader ignites the passion of others for the ministry
and helps them exercise their giftedness. A leader accepts
responsibility, welcomes accountability, holds authority, and

delegates authority according to the distribution of gifted-ness within the team. A leader is one who knows where he or she is going and embraces those who follow him or her. This is not intended to be an exclusive list of qualities of a leader. There are lots more, and there are several wonderful books on leadership within the Christian community.

In terms of leadership within the SPFM, there may be some characteristics that are not so apparent. One of the most important for me is this: personal credibility. Many single parents already feel the church is condescending and judgmental. They will need to see someone in a leadership role with a personal experience that will serve as a testi-mony to the ministry. They will need to see someone who really knows what it feels like to be in their place. To have a leadership team that does not include any single parents will guarantee a short-lived ministry. This person does not need to be the "head honcho," but he or she does need to be visible. I actually recommend people of both genders, who are or have been single parents and who are presently leading exemplary lives, to be part of the teaching team to other single parents. They will bring the credibility to the classes that a person who has never been a single parent cannot possibly bring.

There is another reason why having both genders repre-sented is such a good idea. Most of the single parents who will be interested in participating will be women. Remember that 86 percent of custodial parents are mothers. However, it is very important to have male representation for women to hear and learn about the needs of single dads. Single dads, on the other hand, may not even participate unless there is a man involved. They also need to hear what single mothers are experiencing. The awareness that this opportunity brings to parents of both genders is tremendous.

Once you have prayed about and assembled your leadership team, you may encounter some resistance. Assuming that your church does not have either a singles ministry or a single-parent family ministry, it is only fair to share with you some of the common objections that have been heard from church leadership. I have also shared with you some responses.

- Objection #1: Single parenting is largely the consequence of sin. We don't want to be seen as condoning sinful behavior, and the difficulties are God's way of working out His justice.
- Objection #2: There is little commitment among singles and no dependability.
- Objection #3: Singles ministry ends up being a "meat market" for people looking for a new mate.
- Objection #4: Single-parent families are a big, black hole into which the church will have to pour endless amounts of benevolence. We can't afford it!
- Objection #5: As much as we would like to help, we have to focus on the people who have kept their marriages together. With limited resources, marriage enrichment must be our priority.
- Objection #6: We already have a singles ministry.

It is evident that church leadership feels caught in a real bind. On one hand, they feel they ought to do something to help address and meet the single-adult needs. But on the other hand, they feel threatened. They don't know what to do with single adults, especially single parents. One could infer that ignoring them is the end result of wishing they did not exist. But they do exist and they exist in huge numbers. A realistic recognition of the facts is in order.

- Response #1: There is no doubt that there is sin in divorce and illegitimacy. But neither divorce nor out-of-wedlock birth is an unforgivable sin. Each represents a spiritual paradox. God hates the sin, but He loves His child. These are times in individuals' lives when they are so broken that the prospect of a loving God will finally touch their hearts.

- Response #2: It is a myth that single parents are uncommitted and undependable. Most single parents want only what is best for their children. Unfortunately, they are fed lies and half-truths by the pervading culture and the church; the place where they could find the truth appears not to welcome them into the pews.

- Response #3: Single-parent ministry does not become a "meat market" if parents are encouraged to put their children first and to heal in an affirming and nonjudgmental environment. The truth about the difficulties of blending families must be told. Premarital counseling for remarriage must include heavy doses of reality and should be long-term—six to twelve months—in order to sort through all of the issues.

- Response #4: It is true that single-parent families often have high needs for benevolence. Yet single parents who are encouraged to adjust to their situation and find support in their congregation tend to thrive. Their economics may not always be bright, but Woman at the Well ministry in Woodland Park, Colorado, has monitored tithing among their single mothers in several ministries and reports that 85 percent tithe a full 10 percent.[1] It may be a widow's mite, but God has a way of multiplying mites!

- Response #5: Single parents and their children are today's widows and orphans. There is a biblical mandate to care for them. No one denies the importance of keeping existing marriages strong, but it is not an either-or situation. These two ministries, like many others in the church, can intersect. We will discuss more about that in chapter 12.

- Response #6: This is the clincher: singles ministry is not single-parent family ministry. They are different and they need to be done separately. At least one-half of every single-parent family is a child, and most often, two-thirds. That means, at a minimum, one-half of single-parent family ministry is children's ministry. It's unlikely that you will be able to get that in a singles group!

Influencing Your Senior Pastor

Not every senior pastor has a heart that beats for single-parent family ministry. It's not because he or she is insensitive, but simply because many pastors do not have any personal experience with the issues. For them, it simply doesn't ever come up on the screen. Many pastors, especially those who are older, have been reared in two-parent family homes. Owing perhaps to their personal relationship with Christ, they have experienced better-than-average success in their marriages. Unless their siblings or children were single parents, they may have no personal knowledge from which to draw.

When we couple the lack of personal experience with the nature of the church that tends to deter single parents from the pews, many pastors find they must rely upon articles in *Newsweek* and *Time* to clue them in to the single-parent dilemma. Even then, many of them will say, "We don't have that many single parents in our church."

A single-parent family ministry needs the support of the senior pastor in order to survive. Bearing in mind that care of the widow and the orphan is a biblical mandate, it makes sense to present the theology of single-parent family ministry (which is both implicit and explicit in both the Old and New Testaments) in a loving and dynamic way as a means of influencing the senior pastor's feelings for the ministry. Once the ministry is up and running, provide opportunities for your senior pastor to be involved in the ministry as a guest so that he or she may see the effect that it has on the single-parent families. Share photographs of social occasions and testimonies of parents. If your senior pastor is willing, discuss how some of the language in sermons on Mother's Day and Father's Day might be modified to be sensitive to single-parent issues. In staff meetings, revisit things, such as the drawings on the front of the bulletin or generic mentions from the pulpit about "couples," and consider how single parents might perceive them.

Tenderly nurture a heart for this ministry in your senior pastor so that he or she might loudly proclaim the benefits among colleagues.

12

The Nature of
the Church

WHETHER YOUR CHURCH is large or small, there is a structure that is inherent in each one. Do you operate through an elder board, committees, or some other form of government that is unique to your church? Before you get to that step, it is important to take a look at how your SPFM will function.

By its very nature, SPFM is distinct. Most churches are set up with a number of different spheres of ministry. There is the youth ministry, men's ministry, women's ministry, children's ministry, singles ministry, family ministry, etc. (I know that there are other ministries, such as music, but they don't apply in this case.) The church, for the past several decades, has separated into groups, either by chronological age or by gender. Single-parent family ministry does not necessarily fit neatly into another sphere. In fact, it tends to invade the others. It represents a new paradigm, because it is all of the above. Single-parent family ministry *is* youth ministry, men's ministry, women's ministry, children's ministry, singles ministry, and family ministry.

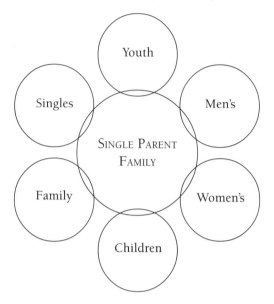

Some of you will have to decide if your SPFM stands alone or if it will fall under one of the other ministries in your church. There is no consensus about where it belongs. Many churches have developed a SPFM out of their singles ministry. Another church may house the SPFM in their congregational-care and outreach ministries. Although there are many options, the following represent the likely possibilities for a single-parent family ministry.

Family Ministry

Single-parent families are, after all, families. They have more in common with two-parent families than they have with singles. However, in the past, churches have defined "family" by a model to which a single-parent family cannot aspire. They struggle to feel whole and adequate. They experience labeling. Not including single-parent families in family ministry further labels them. Putting them in family ministry suggests an order of priorities that is consistent with God's Word.

I have found a church that has expressed reticence in involving single-parent families in their family ministry. One reason they have given is that they are devoted to providing ongoing marriage enrichment opportunities for their married couples. They shared with me that several single parents felt even more failure when hearing about these sessions.

Single parents who are feeling the fresh wounds of betrayal and abandonment need a safe place for themselves. When I suggest that SPFM comes under the headship of the family ministry, I am not suggesting that they be integrated into all of the family ministry's activities immediately. Single-parent families need a place and a season to heal and be restored. We will discuss that more later in this chapter, "Programming with a Purpose."

Children's Ministry

This is another very effective alternative. As I was quick to point out earlier, at least half of every SPFM is children's ministry. Fortunately, many churches have ministries that are for both family and children. Regardless of where the ministry is located within the structure of the church, the children's pastor is critical to the success of the program. Inherent in children's ministry are people who love the kids. Children from single-parent families need lots of people who know their needs and love them unconditionally.

One of the obstacles involved in putting your SPFM under the children's pastor is that a comprehensive ministry involves meeting some very real and often very grim practical needs with which the children's ministry will have difficulty.

Singles Ministry

Many people advocate putting their SPFM under the singles ministry because they already have functioning singles ministry. There is no doubt that is a good reason, especially if there are people in the ministry with a heart for single parents and their children. One of the most important things I would recommend is a survey of your singles group to determine how many of them are single parents with children still at home. My experience indicates that for twenties, thirties, and forties singles groups, the percentage of single parents is shockingly high. I encouraged one singles group in a very large church near me to survey their participants. They found out that 85 percent of their group were single parents! They maintained the SPFM under their singles ministry, but it made a huge difference in their agenda.

Speaking of agenda, I am familiar with a large church that has a policy to discourage single parents from remarriage. I try not to get involved in other churches' policy, but I had to challenge the singles pastors: "If your policy is to discourage remarriage, why do you have the single parents in the singles groups?" In our culture, single parents are rarely encouraged to put their children first. Mixing singles and single parents tends to exacerbate the problem of children falling to the bottom of the priority list.

On the other hand, on of the most beneficial things about having your SPFM under the singles group is that there is already a ministry in place with a budget. Starting from scratch can be a long and difficult experience. Another benefit is that there are many never-married singles and empty-nester singles who are wonderful to have working with this ministry. I have not been able to find a church that can do an effective SPFM without these folks.

Interdenominational Partnership Ministries

I am presently working with a number of small churches in an area where none of them considers itself large enough to do a comprehensive SPFM. They have formed a partnership and work together in their community to minister to single-parent families. In one church, classes are held to teach children and adults new, healthy family life skills, while another church handles the food closet and clothes closet. Still another church administers the benevolence to which they all contribute, etc.

I am excited about the opportunity to develop a model for ministry that works this way. In many communities around the nation, only a cooperative effort among several small churches will produce the kind of ministry that single parents need.

In spite of the fact that your SPFM will probably be housed in one of the other ministries listed above, virtually every ministry can make a contribution to the well-being of a healthy SPFM. When ministries function together, it is a testimony of how God intended His church to be—the Body.

Women's Ministry

An active women's ministry is an ideal way to integrate single mothers into the church. Mentoring takes place in a natural way between older women and younger women. (That sounds biblical!) Unfortunately, most single mothers have to work during the day, and it may be that the women's ministry is simply unavailable to them. Even so, there are lots of ways that the women's ministry can serve the SPFM.

Every year at Christmas, our SPFM hosts a party during which the parents participate in a Christmas-cookie exchange. The tens of dozens of cookies are gifts to the program from the women's ministry. All the parents need to do is load up one of the shirt boxes that has been lined with tissue paper and begin filling it with beautifully decorated Christmas cookies. I wish I could let you hear from this page the *oohs* and *aahs* and the thank-yous that emanate from the room. The children are so excited. The women's ministry tells me that it is one of the highlights of the year. They love to do this service, and their gifts are so appreciated.

Children's Ministry

Sunday-school teachers may be the first adult best friends for many children. Sunday-school teachers have a unique blessing on their lives for teaching the Gospel to these precious youngsters. The goal of the SPFM is to have the children of the single parents involved in Sunday school as often as possible. We know that the majority of Christians give their lives to Jesus while they are yet children. Studies also indicate that in single-parent family homes where a common faith is shared, the family is more likely to avoid the difficult problems associated with single-parent family life.[1]

But some issues may not be obvious. That's why having the pastor of the children's program on board with the SPFM is very important. I try to have the Sunday-school teachers involved in the SPFM training to help them be aware of some of the pitfalls of dealing with children from single-parent family homes.

For children who may be alternating their time between parents on the weekends, it may be impossible for them to be in church every Sunday. Losing rewards for attendance, over which they have no control, defeats and embarrasses them.

Wendy is a little girl of six who characterizes the problem. Her parents were both Christians when they divorced. She alternated weekends with her parents. On Sundays, her mother took Wendy to her church when they were together and her father to his on the weekends she spent time with him. Wendy faithfully attended Sunday school in both churches. At her mother's church, the Sunday-school teacher did not keep track of attendance. But at her father's church, the teacher rewarded the children with bright gold stars on an attendance chart for all to see. When Wendy first noticed that she was missing half of her stars, she complained.

"But you miss every other week," the teacher responded to her.

"No, I don't," she countered. "I go every week."

At that point, the other children sided with the teacher. One little boy said, "That's a lie. You never come!"

Wendy was inconsolable. It took months for her to return to Sunday school at her father's church.

In consulting with churches that are trying to develop a SPFM, I also encourage the children's pastor to find curriculum that does not build week upon week. The absenteeism puts children from single-parent families at a distinct disadvantage when they come into a classroom and find that they are unprepared. The same may be said of memory verses. Another way to promote memorization of Bible verses might be to allow extra time—four weeks instead of two. In that way, children have ample opportunity to be in class and commit their assignment to memory.

I know how difficult it is for children's pastors to recruit Sunday-school teachers. So I pray that there will be no wincing at this suggestion. For many children in single-parent family households, there is no male figure. Children desperately need safe role models in safe places. I cannot think of a better place to have good role models for children from single-parent family homes. Team teaching (with a man and a woman teaching together) is a perfect way to help all children recognize the value of both genders. For children from two-parent homes, it reinforces the family model that they observe day in and day out. For children from single-parent family homes, it provides an opportunity to see men and women work together in positive ways. For them, it may be something that they have never seen before. Team gender teaching is a requirement in the SPFM at our church. One little boy is a perfect example of why I am so strong on this issue.

Steve's father left before he was born. His mother lived with her mother, and for Steve, women were the only authority figures in his life. He had a woman kindergarten teacher, a woman after-school caregiver, two aunts, his mother, and his grandmother. As soon as Steve met his teacher, Joe, he was mesmerized. Joe recounts that Steve hung on his leg like a monkey for the first couple of weeks.

One day, Steve's mother told me they were driving along the freeway when a car pulled alongside of them. The driver looked a lot like Joe. Little Steve began pounding on the window of the car yelling, "Joe! Joe!" The driver in the other car paid no attention and quickly sped by them.

"Honey," his mother said gently, "that wasn't Joe. It's just somebody who looked like him. You really wanted it to be Joe, didn't you?"

"Mom," the little guy said, with tears rolling down his cheeks, "I want everybody to be Joe."

Youth Ministry

Sitting on the floor, rocking back and forth to "Kum Ba Ya" does not cut it in youth ministry anymore. Probably no ministry so well established is changing more rapidly than this one. The Builders and the Boomers may not want change, but the youth group does! What was, in the past, dedicated to competing with the entertainment of the outside world is now leaning toward the small-group concept in which young people can be in relationship with one another. The postmodern world demands authenticity. Today, youth ministry demands biblical adherence, relevance to the world, and integrity to self. Consequently, it has become much more community and service-related.

Many church youth-group members themselves come from single-parent family homes. To be truly effective, a youth pastor or leader needs significant maturity and the awareness of single-parent family issues to help the youngsters face their own pain and struggles as they relate to their spirituality. At the same time, young people from single-parent family homes know from personal experience what it feels like to be abandoned by a parent or to be left to fend for themselves. Young people are drawn to ministry when the church makes it real.

One church with an amazingly ministry-minded youth group has developed a "buddy ministry." Their goal is to pair young people up with single-parent families in which there are much younger children, preferably of the same gender. The youth pastor supervises a meeting between the teen and the single parent where ground rules for the ministry are laid down. It's very simple. The teen commits $1\frac{1}{2}$

hours each week for six months to playing with the children from the single-parent family in the community, at a time when the parent is present. This is not babysitting. The boys can play ball or shoot hoops as they wish. Sometimes the girls do the same types of things, or sometimes they do "girl things."

The ministry has been such a blessing because the families of the youth often get to know the single-parent families. As relationships grow, everyone benefits.

Congregational Care

There is obvious relevance here. Almost every SPFM requires a lot of help from the care ministry. But caution is strongly advised! This ministry, emanating from the compassionate heart of the congregation to meet the most basic of needs, is easily the most misused and abused.

An uncontrolled food closet will resonate with horror stories. Once unethical people become aware of the bounty that is stored there, it becomes like a gold mine that the genie refills in the middle of the night. No matter how much is taken, there is always more. Some of the ethically challenged will sell the products, so generously donated by your congregation, for cash, cigarettes, and yes, drugs. If you give them—the scammers, that is—certificates to buy fresh produce or meat, they may buy one small item and pocket the rest of the cash. I know of one church that, in its mercy, bought shoes for an entire family. Later, a member of the congregation happened to observe the father of the family returning *all* of the shoes for a cash refund! Such occurrences can make one very cynical!

Spiritual issues are at the root of this problem. Anyone who behaves this way does not walk with the Lord. But the spiritual issues lie not only with the abusers; they also lie in the lap of church that allows such behavior. This is a serious case of poor stewardship. According to the parable of the talents, poor stewardship will culminate in future lack. As a congregation, we must not only teach good stewardship to those in need, we must also model it!

An integral piece of truth for the leadership of an SPFM is the realization that needing food from the church is only part of the problem. The real problem is much more complex. Some may not have enough money. They probably don't know how to manage their money. They may be in the wrong job. They may not be walking with the Lord. The financial problem undoubtedly masks a spiritual problem.

Folks in need, need help. But if we try to solve the problem just by treating the symptom, we will be guilty of unfaithfulness ourselves. This is the rule of thumb: Make sure there is accountability. One tactic that has been successfully used by several churches is this: the second time someone asks for food or benevolence, they are also set up with an appointment with a financial counselor. While this may appear to be very time-consuming, it is wise in the long run. Some may not realize that they are wasting their funds. Some just need help getting a better-paying job. Some simply do not make enough, and there is little that can be done immediately. Putting a long-range plan in place gives the individual reason for hope and gives the church the assurance that its resources are not being wasted through bad stewardship.

A comprehensive SPFM will involve some financial counseling or budget classes for single parents. Considering that over 50 percent of single-parent families live in poverty, this should be a given. The leaders/teachers of the SPFM will quickly discover who is most in need, and through their relationship can direct single parents to financial counselors in the church. Two of my most effective counselors were CPA, stay-at-home moms who gave 1½ hours per week to help single mothers with their finances. There were also two men in the church, both of whom came out of personnel positions that helped several single parents find new, better-paying jobs. For the single parents involved in any of the counseling, there was always accountability.

> He who ignores discipline comes to poverty and shame,
> but whoever heeds correction is honored. (Prov. 13:18)

Men's Ministry

This ministry, praise God, has seen an explosion in recent years, thanks in large part to the work of Promise Keepers. As this book earlier stated, men have become confused about their role in society. Many, many men have failed in their responsibility to be husbands and fathers, indicating confusion in their spiritual roles as well. I would recommend that every man in men's ministry read the book *Fatherless America* by David Blankenhorn. This work not only illuminates the most pressing problem in our culture, but I believe it also represents a call to action much like the Book of Nehemiah.

When Nehemiah heard from the men who had traveled to Jerusalem, he wept over the broken-down walls and burnt gates of the city. Every cell in him knew that God had been dishonored and that the city could not stand against the forces of evil with the walls fallen to the ground. Nehemiah prayed, and then God sent him out to begin a major reconstruction project. To rebuild the wall, it does not appear that Nehemiah ordered up anything like a construction crew.

Instead, each section was rebuilt by one man and his family. Together, the entire project was completed by families doing only what was in front of their own homes. In rebuilding the walls of Jerusalem, these men set an example for rebuilding the families in America.

Throughout this nation, millions of children are fatherless. The boys have no one in their lives to show them how to be good men who will one day be husbands and fathers themselves. Without it, many find the modeling they crave in gang leaders. The girls have no father to affirm them in their femininity. They struggle to find male affection and so end up getting it through early sexual adventures. Many of them become pregnant out of wedlock and repeat the cycle again. These children need godly men to influence their lives.

Is it fair to ask men who are busy with their own families to spend time with other children? Let me ask another question. Is it fair that these children, through no fault of their own, do not have father figures? Without the intentional, positive influence of good men and their families, these children will grow up to be men and women who have not been fathered and may one day marry your daughters and sons.

When Nehemiah was ridiculed for his plan, he said, "The God of heaven will give us success" (Neh. 2:20). Looking at the entire project seems overwhelming. But like the families in Nehemiah, we need only do that what is in front of our own house. "'Let us start rebuilding.' So they began this good work" (2:18*b*).

- Encourage men who are considering leaving their families to stick it out, even if it takes years of marriage counseling. Their own sense of personal satisfaction can never justify the legacy they leave to their children in a divorce.

- Encourage men who have already left their families either to reconcile or stay connected to their children. Many noncustodial dads throw up their hands in frustration over the system. Believe me, the system is terrible. Everyone is frustrated. It takes a truly committed man to be there for his children, but the rewards will be great.

  One man who influenced my thinking many years ago made a commitment that he would not remarry until his youngest child was out of high school. He felt that by doing this he was able to really "be there" for his children without interference. He lived nearby, he spent lots of time with them, he attended every sporting and musical event. The outcome is a very, very close relationship. When I hear parents complain about their children, I must remind them: children are children. Parents are supposed to be adults.

- Encourage one another to get involved in the lives of fatherless children in your own neighborhood. Commit to a relationship with a single-parent family. Rebuild the wall in front of your own house.

As you can see, every ministry dealing with people, each of whom are members of some family, has an opportunity to be involved with one another. This is true whether we are talking about single-parent family ministry or another ministry. For this reason, many churches are looking at a reconfiguration of ministry organization. Churches are looking for a new paradigm of pastoral leadership in what is called "family ministry." In attempting to determine where single-parent family ministry would best function, many of us have come to the conclusion that a family pastor would be most efficient. The ministry would include responsibilities to each area I indicated above—women, children, youth, men, single parents, and congregation care. The objective would involve whole-life stewardship and discipleship within a caring community where *family* becomes a verb.

SINGLE-PARENT FAMILY MINISTRY IN A CELL CHURCH

For the past fifteen years, churches have been moving to the *cell,* or small group, concept. The intent has been the establishment of a style more reminiscent of the first-century church. A very large church can employ intimate relational communities within small groups to teach and to disciple. A generic small group may be made up of seniors, younger married parents with children, youth, singles, and custodial and noncustodial parents. It is intended to resemble the makeup and function of an extended family. Members of the group are able to care for the minor needs of everyone within the group. The natural mentoring process benefits both the single parent and his other children.

Every single-parent family has a need to be integrated into a highly relational organism where ministry is done on a one-to-one basis. A single-parent family needs the respect of the other members of the community as they simply love one another. Looking at the single parent as "this month's project" will destroy the trust and safety of the small group.

Most small groups are not designed to be therapeutic. In some cases, a single parent may have more than minor needs. The success of a single-parent family integrating into a group will depend, at least to some degree, upon the functional capabilities of the parent. A very deep need or raw emotion that continues to pour out over a long period of time in the single parent may overwhelm a small group and suck them dry.

There is benefit in allowing a single-parent family to work through some of the issues of their grief, anger, and financial neediness with other single-parent families before they join an integrated small group.

Single-parent family ministry is one of those places where programs just naturally happen. It is a therapeutic ministry much like divorce recovery or a twelve-step program—a place designed to meet acute needs. A SPFM can become an effective outreach for the church, where single-parent families will eventually move into a small group of their own.

In 1 Timothy 5, Paul leaves instruction for a ministry model to be used at the church in Ephesus in caring for those—specifically widows—with acute needs. It replicates the system used in Jerusalem in Acts 6:1 to feed the widows who had no one else to care for them. Even in the first century, a therapeutic ministry intervened for those who had higher than normal needs. That is the purpose of a SPFM program.

PROGRAMMING WITH A PURPOSE

The SPFM program is a tool that churches use to provide entry points for single-parent families. For the 95 percent of single-parent families outside the church, there is little opportunity to build a relationship until they come in the door. A needs-driven SPFM is probably one of the most effective ways of encouraging unchurched single-parent families into the building. At a time when some single-parent families are dropping out of church, a SPFM gives them a reason to drop in.

To Whom?

The first order of business will be to decide where your SPFM will direct its energy. To whom should you minister? The congregation? The community? I have already given my reasons for considering outreach into the community: 95 percent of single-parent families are beyond the walls of your church, beyond the grasp of your home groups, and beyond the hearing of the gospel.

In a two-year study completed on a church ministry to single-parent families, more than half of the families who were unchurched (about 60 percent) regularly started attending church as a result of the program. Many reported that they had never considered the church to be a safe place for them. Neither had they ever considered it to be a source of support. What happened? Their needs were met. They found the church to be accepting and loving. Through welfare, the government has done a tremendous job of eradicating from the minds of most folks the idea that the church is a source of support and community. When single parents see that the church is relevant to them, they come.

Should your ministry be to single parents only, to children of single parents only, or to the whole family? Have you noticed that this book has consistently called for single-parent *family* ministry? Families in crisis must be treated holistically. Having parents and children on the same page, so to speak, promotes faster healing. Children are not as resilient as once thought. They are especially vulnerable to falling through the cracks. Teaching healthy life skills to children of single-parent families is equally as important as teaching the parents.

Mission Statement

What is the mission statement that reflects the direction of your ministry? A mission statement functions as a verbal map so that everyone knows where they are going and how they are going to get there. Every ministry will have its own because every church will have a unique ministry. The mission statement should be developed when the leadership team has pulled together and the group is beginning to outline the direction. The goals should be directly related to the mission statement and the needs of the population you will be serving.

When?

When is the most convenient time for your SPFM to meet? The decision concerning the time of the day and week that the SPFM will meet is one of the most important that will be made. It must be convenient for most single-parent families. Here are some things to keep in mind.

Forget about weekdays. Single parents have to work. Weeknights are best *if* the program finishes early enough so that very young children can get home and get to bed and school-age children have time to do their homework. Programs that last beyond 7:30 P.M. are counterproductive to the values necessary for a healthy family. It is critical to remove obstacles from the path of the single parent. A program that runs too late is a major obstacle.

A program that requires more work for the single parent is an obstacle. A very effective method of removing the dinner obstacle for single-parent families on a weeknight is the provision of dinner for the whole family around 5:30 or 6:00 P.M., followed by the program. This timing allows most parents to get off work, pick up their children, and go straight to the church for dinner. Experience indicates that if parents have time to go home between picking up their children and going to a class, they are not likely to go out again; it is too much trouble. By providing a meal, a major obstacle to their participation is eliminated. They have time to relax, and they have an opportunity to build community with the other families.

Saturday mornings or afternoons are typically out of the question for single-parent families. They usually have too much to do in terms of keeping up with housework and children's athletics. Saturday nights are usually reserved for social activities with friends. In order to see if Saturday night will work, you will need to survey your group. Sunday mornings work well for a support group for the parents while children are in their regularly scheduled Sunday school classes.

What Format?

Why have you chosen the format you have? Every church will have a ministry that is unique. That's the way it should be. God calls each church to a particular kind of ministry. The giftedness and passion of the leadership and volunteers involved will determine how the ministry comes together. Considering the long list of needs that SPFM represents, your question needs to be: How many of the following components do you want to do or are you capable of handling?

I. Bible study: cell groups or Sunday morning Sunday school

II. Emotional healing:

   A. *Support groups*—can be the focus of the Sunday school hour
   B. *Counseling*—provide lay counseling or funds for professional counseling

III. Physical needs:

A. *Childcare*—perhaps church has a daycare center or has funds to help single parents pay the high cost of childcare. Consider a network among single parents themselves.

B. *Food closet*—available to single parents at times other than during the day. May also include special holiday food baskets for single-parent families.

C. *Clothing ministry*—both parents and children need clothes. Exchange ministry or arrange with a consignment shop. Also, consider referrals to outside agencies.

D. *Housing*—household maintenance and repair is an overwhelming task for single-parent families. A handyman ministry is ideal and incorporates other ministries in the congregation. Lack of finances are usually crucial. Recommend a special benevolence fund for security deposits, etc. Some parents may need ongoing help with their rent until they can get back on their feet.

E. *Automobile*—Even routine maintenance is a problem. Car care ministries are a great way to involve men and youth ministries. It could also involve finding used cars for single parents with little or no funds.

IV. Life Skills

A. *Budget and money management*—Christian Financial Concepts has an excellent single-parent workbook and workbooks for children and teens.

B. *Parenting skill*—the video class *Parenting with Love and Logic* is highly recommended. Also, *Systematic Training for Effective Parenting* (STEP).

C. *Communication Skills*—the inability to effectively communicate destroys relationships with family and friends. Conflict-resolution skills ease tensions with an ex-spouse, teens, and coworkers. Professionals consider *Core Communication* to be the best in the field.

D. *New job skills*—a program or money to help retrain or provide brush-up classes. May include job search ministry.

13

GOALS AND OBJECTIVES
OF SPFM

A SPFM WILL BE EFFECTIVE only if it truly believes in the inherent value of the single parent. God did not error when He made this person. He is not disgusted that this woman or man is a single parent, that a divorce has occurred, or that a child has been born out of wedlock. The single parent has not stripped them of his or her giftedness because they have sinned. God's love covers everyone, and His sacrifice redeems anyone who has faith in Him. Jesus' own ministry was to tax collectors and prostitutes—people that disgusted others. But Jesus saw in them what they were created to be.

When I meet a single parent, particularly one in a real crisis, I ask God to allow me to see that person as He sees him or her: not as a wretched sinner, but as He intended for them to be. That is how He saw Matthew the tax collector, Mary the prostitute, and Saul the persecutor of the church.

Pray for this discernment so that you will be able to minister to the person God intended instead of what is standing before you. Learning to look at a person and see what God sees will leave your heart full of love for that individual. It is the enemy that prowls about like a lion seeking to devour and destroy. God wants them to be saved. God wants them to be what He intended, and our goal is simply to be Jesus in their lives.

Beware of recovery programs that do not teach new life skills. I know of many people, including single parents, who have become addicted to recovery. Unless they teach new life skills, they tend to keep people negatively focused on their problems.

Many churches offer divorce recovery programs. If they teach some new skills, they can be very effective by helping to address the pain and emotional baggage in the lives of the adults. Children need emotional healing too. Most divorce recovery programs do not minister to the children. Furthermore, divorce represents less than 40 percent of single parents in the community. What about the other 60 percent?

Unfortunately, many divorce recovery programs consider successful completion to mean that the individual believes he or she is ready for a new relationship. Three to five years is actually what it takes for most people to work through the grief process. Most single parents remarry far too quickly. Not only do they take their unresolved issues into the next relationship, they hinder the plan God has for them and for their children. They do not wait upon the Lord. Single parents must be taught the importance of putting their children first. Unless they do, they will very likely repeat the divorce process within a few more years.

An individual six-week program or a twelve-week program, no matter how good it is, will not be enough. The objective is to keep single-parent families in community until they have had a realistic chance to heal and build new life skills. Those things take time. Effective programming combines three or four different skill-building programs into the academic year. For example, I use a twelve-week program designed to build healthy family systems during the fall quarter. The one that I use is one I wrote myself, called *1 Parent + Kids*. I wrote it because I was unable to find a program to fit the needs I was hearing from the single parents who wanted to participate. It is not a divorce recovery program. The material is designed to apply to all single parents, whether they are divorced, never married, widowed, or abandoned.

In the first four weeks, the parents are able to look at the issues they face as single parents—including the grief cycle and their family of origin—for clues as to their past and present behavior. They are also able to take a look at their children's development and grief. The remainder of the program deals with new life skills that form the elements of a healthy family structure. Those elements are defined as appreciation or respect, commitment, communication, flexibility or adaptability, spirituality, and time together.

That program is followed with a six-week parenting program. *Parenting with Love and Logic* is excellent. The goal is to equip parents with more skills. Single mothers may have a difficult time with their children, especially adolescent sons. They may have never considered themselves to be disciplinarians, or they may feel weak in that role. Likewise, fathers may have a difficult time nurturing their children. All parents, but especially single parents, do better with systematic skills that teach them how to effectively use consequences instead of their voice or their hand to raise responsible children.

A four-week financial workshop allows each person's budgeting and money managing to get personal attention from a certified financial counselor. Most financially struggling single parents recognize that they need help, but they are often too embarrassed to come into a class. In our society, the notion that finances are very private is a deeply entrenched idea. To overcome that reticence, to provide a place where parents feel safe to be open and honest, the financial workshops are scheduled second or third in the line up.

A woman who teaches finances to single parents in a local community center uses an intriguing tactic. She develops the atmosphere of an investment club. Financial issues are not embarrassing or secret, because the facilitator carefully reinforces the idea that the amount of money that they have does not reflect upon them personally as either a success or failure. Money is simply viewed as a tool used to get from one place to another. The goals of the group become much more important. They brainstorm their very real problems, and they calculate as a group the progress that they make as a real investment club would do.

The final segment that I use is a communication-skills class. *Core Communication* is favored by many counselors and other mental health professionals. Everyone can benefit from this kind of instruction. What we know from studies of single parents is that most people who are divorced or unwed come from families that were also divorced or unwed. The consequence of the instability in their lives is that they have likely never learned effective communication skills. A good communication-skills class can help individuals learn to take responsibility for their speech. It helps control conflict and develop skills to reach resolution. The parents that have participated in these classes list them as critical to their healing and future well-being.

There is no hard and fast rule about the order of these programs, except as I mentioned earlier concerning the financial workshop: Pay attention to the school calendar! This is important when scheduling all single-parent classes. Don't expect families to show up over holidays or breaks. Giving families two to four weeks between some of the classes is also very effective.

The objective in utilizing four different modules is multifaceted. First, parents want and need more information than can be presented in a single program. Every class will empower and encourage them. Second, parents want and need more than twelve weeks to build community within the church and with the other parents in their class. Third, the longer period of time gives everyone in the class opportunities to observe growth and change in themselves, growth in others, and recognize the power in those changes. Fourth, four classes give new parents four different entry points. Although the classes do not build on one another, per se, they each offer information related to issues of parenting and functional family life skills.

In order for a family system to function well, everyone in the family needs to be on the same page. It is critical that all four modules have parallel classes for the children in their appropriate age groups. I had to write a children's curriculum to accompany the material that I presented to the parents. (Publication of that material is in the works.) The outcome of the year-long program produces such significant changes in the families that I included some of the interviews in the appendix from parents involved in the two-year study.

Social times help build a sense of belonging to a community for both parents and children. They also provide a venue for other members of the congregation to participate in good times. Having other members of the congregation participate, and creating situations where single-parent families get to know other families in the church, encourages single-parent families to attend church. The rule of relationship evangelism is that new people will come back to church when they know they will see three or four friends. The other wonderful thing that occurs is the willingness of two-parent families to become advocates to the congregation for single parents and the ministry.

Each of these components contributes to the well-being of the family. Healthy family skills have not kept pace with the fast-moving role changes between the genders that have put mothers into the breadwinner circle and have put fathers out to pasture. It is unlikely that, as a society, we will be able to put this toothpaste back in the tube. I am not sure that anyone really wants to. Therefore, how will we deal with it? Will the humanistic, secular society develop new models of family for us, or will the Body of Christ get out of its holy huddle and teach a healthy family system that works in postmodern America?

14

VOLUNTEERS
AND DOLLARS

RECRUITING VOLUNTEERS FOR YOUR SPFM

BUILDING AWARENESS of the need is the first step. In some churches, the recruitment consists of casting the "big net." Announcements can be made from the pulpit or a notice can go into the bulletin. This is standard for children's Sunday school teacher recruitment. If it works for Sunday school, the assumption is that it will work for SPFM.

Warning: It may not. Single-parent family ministry is new. People have no idea what to expect when they volunteer. One almost always knows at least some part of the job description for Sunday school or childcare, but this is a brand new field of ministry. People are apprehensive.

Before you recruit even one volunteer teacher, the team needs to know the perimeters of the program. Earlier, we talked about the time of the program. The time that is chosen will have some effect upon the volunteers that you can count on. If it is on a weeknight, which is preferable for most single parents, the adult Sunday school groups are an excellent resource. It is more effective to recruit from smaller groups, instead of trying to raise volunteers out of the congregation at large.

One Sunday morning, before I was to make a presentation to several of the Sunday school groups for volunteers for the SPFM, the Lord gave me an idea. It involved appealing to the sense of intimacy almost everyone has with a single-parent family these days. As I have said before, people rarely recognize the widespread seriousness of the problem but almost everyone knows a single-parent family.

I spoke briefly about the plans for the single-parent ministry. Then, one by one, I asked how many people had been raised in a single-parent family; how many were or had been single parents themselves; how many had children, siblings, or other relatives that were single parents; and finally, how many had friends or neighbors that were single parents. Virtually everyone raised his hand at one or more points. As I went from class to class, I made mental notes (that were quickly put on paper once I left the room), particularly on those who had grown up in a single-parent family home and those older couples who had grandchildren in a single-parent family home. Those folks became the backbone for my volunteer staff. Their heart was in the program from the beginning.

The process that I used to connect them to the program was critical. The following week, I took my notes and made phone calls to individuals. I asked them to consider their involvement in the program and said that if they were interested, we would make an appointment to have coffee and they could take a look at the curriculum. When we were able to meet and each person had a chance to view the curriculum and talk about their own experiences with single parenting, they almost always expressed a desire to be involved. The recruiting was time consuming; but most people stay involved much longer when their personal experience gives them a high motivation.

On occasion, one of the volunteers would tell me about someone else who expressed interest. Through a wide network the program has always been fully staffed, sometimes with more than I actually need.

Screening and training volunteers is an integral part of the process. Screening is not simply for the purpose of weeding out those that may not be able to work with the team for various reasons, but it also allows individuals to work within their areas of giftedness. Not everyone interested in the program will be a teacher. That's good. All gifts are necessary—leadership, administration, hospitality (making sure those social occasions happen), counseling, mercy, and helps (handling the practical aspects of the ministry), exhortation (writing notes of encouragement and making phone calls), and—last but not least—prayer.

MONEY FOR THE SPFM

A comprehensive single-parent family ministry will require at least a part-time staff person (depending upon the size and scope of the ministry) and a funded budget. Remember that 53 percent of single parents live below the poverty level. Expecting single-parent families to foot the bill exclusively or to staff the ministry is to take a walk in la-la land. Many single parents cannot afford to pay for the materials or any of the help that may be a part of the ministry. Their time is very limited, so it is nonproductive to assume they can be part of the volunteer staff. Keep in mind that single parents are the end user of the ministry. They will not be able to use it when they most need it if they are expected to do it.

> At the end of every three years, bring all the tithes of that year's produce and store it in your towns, so that the Levites (who have no allotment or inheritance of their own) and the aliens, the fatherless and the widows who live in your towns may come and eat and be satisfied, and so that the Lord you God may bless you in all the work of your hands. (Deut. 14:28–29)

The Bible is rather direct about the use of the tithe. Fully one-third was to be set aside to give to the Levite priests, the aliens, and the widows and orphans. In spite of that passage, you may have some difficulty finding financing for your ministry. Missions budgets, a children's or family ministry, a single's ministry, and care ministries may all be sources of funding for the SPFM. You will need it. Curriculum can be costly. All of the programs in a multiple module concept will add to the start-up expenses. However, once purchased, these materials can be used over and over again. If there are some additional costs associated with the facility, be sure to add them in as well.

If your church cannot, or will not, come up with the full amount of money required, find out from the governing board if it is possible to raise funds for ministry. Creative fundraising may produce the money necessary to continue. Ask for monetary donations from the congregation for specific events, either in the bulletin or through the newsletter.

Learn what services are available from the community. Many supermarkets are willing to cooperate and donate food to church organizations. Coffee shops (Starbucks is wonderful for this) will donate day-old coffee to your ministry. Local theaters, sports teams, special events, etc., often will have discounted tickets available for single parents with children. Find someone who can call and ask about these things.

Your staff person should know what community services are available to assist with emergencies. Utility companies often have plans to help with low-income people when they are behind on their bills. Many communities have emergency funds to assist with this sort of need. Talk to local newspapers about running a story on the single-parent ministry and speak about specific needs that must be met. Most often, help will come in.

For a church that wants to begin a SPFM before there is money in the budget to do it, the best place to start is a Sunday school support group. This basically requires no program, no volunteers, and very little money. Materials for the class may be available through adult CE. The objective, while the children are in Sunday school, is to simply provide a space to get to know one another and support one another through the difficult times. Then, commence planning with a larger goal in mind. Begin working on a submittal for the budget committee at least six months before the new fiscal year.

One word of warning: It is conceivable that the SPFM could become one of the largest ministries in your church, especially if you are willing to reach outside the walls to bring in some of that 95 percent.

CONCLUSION

Remember the Singles Again Support Group that I mentioned was our church's first attempt at SPFM so long ago? I will never forget one man as he shared about the single parents in that group. "When the single parents first came into the church, the whole ministry could be represented by a box of tissues." He said, as he held up a box of Kleenex. "In the early weeks and months, there were a lot of tears shed. Those of us who were there didn't know what to do. We just told them that God loved them and that He had a plan for their lives. Mostly, we just listened and cried with them and laughed with them.

"In a few months, there was more laughing than crying. Within a couple of years later, a miracle had occurred. The box of tissues was gone. It was replaced by an apron. Their willingness to serve has changed our church and our community."

God changed those single parents, one of whom was myself. God has ministry designed into each person. Helping someone that is broken and hurting is not enabling them; it is walking alongside of them so that God can help them discover where their purpose lies. An effective SPFM will return to your church many times over the effort that has been put into it.

APPENDIX

THE FOLLOWING ARE INTERVIEWS conducted with participants of the single-parent family ministry program. These were completed for the study done to determine the effectiveness of *1 Parent + Kids* curriculum in helping parents resolve their personal issues, raise their sense of personal parental adequacy, and discover the church as a safe community for them and their children. I have included the interviews to share with the reader some of the feedback I have been privileged to hear. These interviews are from real people, although the names have been changed for their protection. Along with the hundreds of personal reports, they are testimony to the tremendous influence the ministry has on single-parent families.

☩   ☩   ☩

"Probably one of the most important aspects of the program for me has been the realization that the church could be, and should be, a source of support for my son and me. I was always afraid of becoming ill and not being able to be there for my son. Having the support of my church family gave me a heightened sense of confidence. I had been fearful of the church and had considered that they would be too judgmental of my situation. Until I heard you relate some of the statistics regarding divorce among the churched and really encourage the class to invest themselves in their church home, I considered church to be the last place to find support. I will never forget the day, sometime during the class, that I said to myself, *I can do this*. When I stopped being scared, Cameron stopped being scared too. Now that I am confident and happy, Cameron is also confident and happy. I don't know about remarriage; I know I will be very careful."

—Cynthia P.

(This parent has very recently remarried. She married a man from the church who had never been married before. She related that she had felt very cautious and remained friends for more than a year before considering marriage. They prepared themselves with an additional year of premarital counseling.)

"For me, the class provided a sense of being supported in my feelings. Even though I had actually been divorced for some time, I had not allowed my daughter to process it. The idea that my daughter would benefit from talking to other adults about the difficulties she was having with her father had not occurred to me. Maryellen felt very affirmed by her experience with the teachers. My experience was also very positive. I have begun going to church. We have even moved to be closer to it. Maryellen is enjoying the youth program. I would not have done that if you had not encouraged us so strongly to find a home church. I don't know if I will ever remarry. I think I would like to, but Maryellen is the first priority. I am looking at things very differently than I did before with regard to remarriage."

—Jessica L.

"We all loved the program. My kids really loved it. They could hardly wait to go. It gave us so many opportunities to talk about the hard things in easy ways. I really appreciated how easy it was to discuss things with them after the classes. One of the things that I really liked was the opportunity to connect with other single parents and feel so supported. We brainstormed problems in our small groups, and I started thinking in some new ways. We have also started going to church again. That is because of the program. It has really contributed to our sense of well-being. I don't know if I will ever remarry. It doesn't really matter. I am so busy with work and with the kids, and we are doing very well. If it happens, OK, but I am not looking."

—Susan R.

"I am just beginning to feel some comfort about being a single parent. The class came just weeks after our separation, and I was really raw. I see now so many of the issues and questions that I had were addressed by the program. Knowing that other people were going through the same thing and [realizing] that I was normal was very affirming. I came away from the class feeling encouraged that my parenting skills were adequate to do a good job as a single parent. My goal is for my sons to have a good relationship with their father. My anger has really dissipated as a result of the class, but his has not. The class gave me a real step up, in terms of getting a handle on what was going on for me and for the children."

—Paulette J.

"The classes were a very positive experience for both Robert and myself. I got so many great ideas. Because I had never been married, I didn't realize that I had so many issues, but I could see that my anger over Robert's father abandoning us and not paying any child support was very similar. I didn't realize I had so much to work through. The class provided a great support system. It gave me incredible confidence that I can do all right if I am on my own. I am finally off welfare. We'll never be rich, but we will be OK. Robert loved it! It has really improved our communication. I feel now that we can freely share. The classes really made me see myself as a valuable, capable, person and I am kinda enjoying that right now."

—Judith B.

"The classes were wonderful for my sons. They loved their teachers. Both boys have not known their father because he left when I was pregnant with the youngest. I don't know if he is dead or alive. The boys have no good, male role models, and having men in the class has been the best. They have had a chance to see how men behave. The class gave me so much con- fidence that I could actually be a good parent that I have taken other parenting classes to improve my skills. That has opened up the door to other relationships and other ideas. I have started going to a church near our house. I believe that God cares about me and loves my sons and me and wants the best for us. That is new thinking for me. I'm not sure if I will remarry. I am finding that I am happier now than I have ever been, and since I see myself as a good parent, I don't think I really need to. I would really like to find some good men to be mentors for my sons, though.

—Pamela M.

"I can't even begin to tell you how beneficial it was to me. Since I am Jewish, I was really worried that I would hear things that are offensive to me, but, that never happened. In fact, I felt very affirmed about my going to synagogue. I have told several of my friends about it. In fact, one day there were several of us who had separated or divorced sitting around, talking about it in kind of a workshop setting. Some of them had been divorced for several years. I realized that I was light years ahead of them in coping with the situation, because of the class. Natalie loved it. One day she saw her teacher in the grocery store, and she couldn't stop talking about it. It was very positive for both of us. I am overwhelmed at the quality of program that your church does for the community. It has truly impressed me. Because of the class, I am much more relaxed about my parenting and about having Natalie see her father."

—Marian T.

"The program was very positive for me. I have not known any other single dads, and it was very helpful for me to see other men in this role as well. I had a much better appreciation of what my children were going through, because of the classes. It has helped all of us open up to one another. The most important thing that I have done is to become more flexible in my parenting. The class helped me understand that some of my expectations were unreasonable. The kids have relaxed, and I feel so much more confident. We recently redecorated my daughter's room, and she was thrilled. Before the class, before I understood what she was experiencing, I would not have permitted that. I am very pleased with the changes I have made. We are all going to church at least twice a month, and we have committed to making it an important part of our lives. I have dated in the past, but I don't really want to now. I want to spend my time with the kids. And I am really trying to encourage them to spend some time with their mother, too."

—James S.

"My son Rick and I really enjoyed the program. It gave me an opportunity to think in new ways. My most memorable moment came early in the program when I heard that I alone was responsible for the outcome of my child. Hoping that someone would come along and bail me out was faulty thinking. It gave me permission to make the commitment that I needed to make and to do the things that I needed to do for Rick's long-term welfare. By the time the program was over, I had tremendous self-confidence that I could do it alone. Before, I was terrified that I would not be able to raise my son by myself. We are going to church—not a lot, but we didn't go at all before. Rick really likes Sunday school, and I am much more comfortable than I used to be. I don't really know how I feel about God. I was dating someone with children, but the relationship has ended because I was able to recognize the potential problems of putting the two families together. Without the program, I would have been looking for very different things in a mate than I am now."

—Jenny C.

"The class has had a very positive effect upon my parenting. My ex-wife has always told me that I am a terrible parent. To some degree, she may have been right, but I think I am much better at it now. I feel much more confident. I really appreciated knowing what my children were going through. Dina loved the classes. She is always eager to come back to church with me. It has provided a very positive experience for her and church. David Jr. and I are still having problems, but because of the class, I have been able to lighten up a bit. He says that he still thinks that I am a jerk. I like to date, and dating helps me with my self-esteem. The information about remarriage is very scary, but I think that marriage is a way to get over the issue of feeling like a failure. If I ever do remarry, it will be because we have done a lot of premarital counseling."

—David D.

"The program was really valuable for me. It helped me to understand the process of what I was going through. The information was pertinent. It brought the feelings that I had into perspective. Some people think that because you haven't married, the feelings are different than being divorced. They are not. I thought we would get married! I feel abandoned too. I was really grateful that you allowed those of us who had not been married into the class. I felt welcomed and loved and valued. I never felt judged. I am definitely a better parent. You really encouraged us to be good parents and to make good decisions from here on out for our children and ourselves. I came away believing that God loves me. Both Adam and I love coming to church. Adam loves to see his teacher on Sunday, and it has been so positive for someone in church to call his name and pick him up and hug him. I think that I would like to get married someday, but if I do, it will be for the right reasons. Thinking that I needed someone to take care of me got me into this situation. I don't plan to make that mistake again."

—Stephanie J.

"I had been separated from my husband for several years prior to coming to the class. I didn't really expect much in the way of healing, but I found that it was very good for me to hear other people's stories and to be able to learn from them. Even though life was good before coming, I realize now that I was sad all of the time. I felt stuck and thought that was the way life would always be for me. The most important piece for me has been the realization that, even though I am the one that filed for the divorce, my husband left me years before with his addictive drug use. I felt freed from the guilt and have been so much happier since the classes. I am much more optimistic, and I am confident that we can get on with our lives. The kids are much happier too. I also feel so much better about setting boundaries around the behavior of my ex and my children. I

always felt just helpless before, but this class gave me the confidence that I could be an excellent parent."
—Kathleen A.

"This was my second divorce. I made every mistake you cautioned against after the first one. Remarriage was a high priority for me. I felt like such a failure, and my fear of trying to raise my son alone encouraged me to remarry within two years. My second husband was more controlling than my first. The second divorce has left me in far worse shape financially and emotionally than the first one did. I can testify that my oldest son had far more discipline problems after my second marriage than when we were living alone. He has since gone to live with his father, and I am not sure that I have not lost him! After the second divorce, I felt very isolated. My second husband was very active in the church and a very popular, charismatic person. I felt blamed. There are still members in the church who shun me. That really hurts, but I can see other single parents who have experienced similar things, and I recognize that I am not alone. My parenting skills and my patience have improved since taking the classes. My priorities have changed. My two young sons have really benefited. I don't know if I will remarry. I think I would like to because I don't want to be alone, but I am worried about making another mistake."
—Carole M.

"The program helped my boys and me work through our anger and our sense of hopelessness. The separation was very fresh when we began, and I don't think that we would have managed as well as we did without it. I always felt very supported—financially and emotionally—by the church. Even though there were a lot of problems staying in the church where my former in-laws attend, I felt love and an encouragement to stay for the sake of my children. The boys know that they can depend upon people there because the class is so connected to the church in their minds. I learned more about parenting than I ever had before. It never occurred to me that there were actual elements of a healthy family. It feels much easier now to determine if I am doing the right thing or the wrong thing for my kids. For example, I recognized that there were some things that I had been doing that undermined the sense of loyalty to the family for them. I would have never known that. I feel very confident that we are on the right track. The only time I think about remarriage is when I feel so overwhelmed by the financial stuff. But I recall I was overwhelmed by financial stuff when I was married. Right now I think bringing in another person into our house with two boys who are preadolescent and a teenage girl would be a catastrophe. After they are out of school, I will consider it."

—Debbie J.

ENDNOTES

CHAPTER 1

1 Barbara Defoe Whitehead, *The Divorce Culture, 1997, Alfred A. Knopf,* New York, N.Y. pp. 13–50.
2 *Christianity Today*, "Churchmen Unite in War on Poverty," Vol. 10, Oct. 1965–March 1966, p. 482.
3 Paul Johnson, *A History of the American People,* 1997, Harper Collins, New York, N.Y., p. 876.
4 Whitehead, p. 3.

CHAPTER 2

1 *Solo*, March–April, 1982, p. 38
2 *Current Population Reports,* pp. 20–483, 1995, U.S. Census
3 David Blankenhorn's book, *Fatherless America,* Basic Books, 1995, is a "must read" on this subject.
4 Associated Press, AOL, Thursday, August 7, 1997.
5 "The Faces of Single Parenting," *Single Parent Family* Magazine, October 1994.
6 *Dear Dad: The Owner's Guide to Single-Fathering*, Patrick Batchelder, p. 5.
7 David Elkind, *The Hurried Child,* Addison Wesley, 1988, 1981.

8   Sara McLanahan and Gary Sandefur, *Growing Up With a Single Parent: What Hurts, What Helps*, Harvard University Press, Cambridge, Mass., 1994, p. 25.

9   Kurdek, Fine, et. al., *"School Adjustment in 6th Graders: Parenting Transitions, Family Climate, and Peer Norm Effects, Child Development, Child Development"*, (1995): pp. 432–443.

10 David Blankenhorn, *Fatherless America*, Basic Books, New York, N.Y,. 1995, pp. 26–32.

11 *Current Population Reports,* pp. 20–483, 1995, U.S. Census

12 "Better Family Values," Christianity Today, America Online, 1995.

13 Whitehead, p. 8.

14 Nancy Palmer and Ana Tangel-Rodriguez, *When Your Ex Won't Pay,* Pinon Press, Colorado Springs, Co., 1995, p. 9.

15 Robert Emery, *Marriage, Divorce and Children's Adjustment,* Sage Pub., 1988, Newbury Park, California, p. 26.

16 Stepfamily Association of America publications, 1997, 1800-735-0329.

17 Whitehead, p. 130.

18 "The Diversity and Strength of American Families," Hearing, Select Committee on Children, Youth and Families, Ninety-ninth Congress, Second Session, February 25, 1986 (Washington D.C.: U.S. Government Printing Office, 1986), 74.

19 Whitehead, p. 130.

20 Lynn White, *"Growing Up With Single Parents and Stepparents: Long Term Effects on Family Solidarity,"* Journal of Marriage and the Family, 56, (1994): 935–948.

21 Don Swenson, "A Model of the Remarried Family," *Journal of Divorce and Remarriage,* Vol. 27 (1/2), 1997, pp. 159–180.

22 Bob Sipchen, *Seattle Times* staff writer. Interview reported in *Seattle Times, "Divided on Divorce,"* February 24, 1997.

23 Andrew J. Cherlin, Frank F. Furstenberg, Jr., *"Stepfamilies in the United States: A Reconsideration,"* Annual Review, Sociological, 1994, 20:359–81

24 Dobson, Dr. James, *Focus on the Family* newsletter, September 1995, p. 2.

25 McCall and Land, *"Trends in While Male Adolescent, Young Adult and Elderly Suicide: Are there underlying structural factors?"* Social Science Register, Vol. 23 (1994) pp. 57–81.

26 *"Extra curricular Activities and High School Dropouts;"* Sociology of Education, Vol. 68, (1995): p. 57–81.

27 Alan Booth and Paul Amato, "Parental Gender Role Non tradition-alism and Offspring Outcomes," Jrl. of Marriage and the Family, Vol. 56, (1994), pp. 865–877.

28 Robert Bolgar, Hallie Zweig-Frank, and Joel Paris, "Childhood Antecedents of Interpersonal Problems in Young Adult children of Divorce," Journal of the American Academy of Child and Adolescent Psychiatry, Vol 34, (1995): pp. 143–150.

29 Frank Furstenberg, Jr. and Julien O. Teitler, ™"Reconsidering the Effects of Marital Disruption: What Happens to Children of Divorce in Early Adulthood?" Journal of Family Issues, Vol. 15 (1994): 173–190.

30 "Welfare Reform: Advocates of the Republican Plan," World News Tonight With Peter Jennings, Jan. 12, 1995. America On Line

31 Virginia Thabes, "A Survey Analysis of Women's Long-Term, Postdivorce Adjustment," Journal of Divorce & Remarriage, Vol. 27, 1997, (3/4)

32 Whitehead, p. 105.

33 Blankenhorn, p.16.

CHAPTER 3

1 Leslie Margolin, "Child Abuse by Mother's Boyfriends: Why the overrepresentation?" Child Abuse and Neglect, Vol. 16 (1992), pp. 541–552.

2 E.M. Hetherington and W.G. Clingempeel, eds. "Coping with Marital Transitions," Monogr. Soc. Res. Child Development. Vol. 57, Nos. 2–3.

CHAPTER 4

1 Mark Fine and Lawrence Kurdek, "Parenting Cognitions in Stepfamilies: Differences Between Parents and Stepparents and Relations to Parenting Satisfaction," Journal of Social and Personal Relationships, Vol. 11 (1994): p. 95–112.

2 Esther Wald, The Remarried Family, Family Service Assoc. of America, New York, N.Y., p. 46.

3 Cheryl Pruett et al., "Social Support Received by Children in Stepmother, Stepfather, and Intact Families," The Journal of Divorce and Remarriage, vol. 19, (1993): p. 165–179.

4 James Bray, et al., "Longitudinal Changes in Stepfamilies: Impact on Children's Adjustment," Paper presented Aug. 15, 1992, annual meeting of American Psychological Assoc., Washington, D.C.
5 Fine and Kurdek, pp. 95–112.
6 Robert Emery, p. 32.
7 Lawrence Kurdek, "Predicting Marital Dissolution: A 5-Year Prospective Longitudinal Study of Newlywed Couples," Journal of Personality and Social Psychology, Vol. 64, (1994): pp. 221–242.
8 Cherlin and Furstenberg, _Stepfamilies in the United States, A Reconsideration,_ p. 374.
9 This is a term coined to express the loss of parental bonding that occurs when both parents (usually in the case of a divorce) refocus their attention from the marriage and the needs of the family unit to their personal satisfaction.
10 Interview conducted May 1997, Bellevue, Washington.
11 Candan Duran-Adydintug, "Children of Divorce Revisited: When They Speak Up." Journal of Divorce & Remarriage, Vol. 27 (1/2), 1997.

CHAPTER 5

1 Andrea Stolba and Paul Amato, "Extended Single Parent Households and Children's Behavior," The Sociological Quarterly, Vol. 34, (1993) pp. 543–549.
2 Stable: 2 "Parent Families and Troubled Teens.," 1990, April, _St. Louis Dispatch,_ quoted by Nancy Morrison, _"Successful Single Parent Families," Journal of Divorce & Remarriage,_ Vol. 22, 1995,pp. 205–219.
3 Morrison, p. 206.
4 Morrison, p. 215.
5 Morrison, p. 207.

CHAPTER 6

1 Sarah Pomeroy, _Goddesses, Whores, Wives, and Slaves._ Schocken Books, New York, 1976, p. 5.
2 Bonnie Bowman Thurston, _The Widows, A Women's Ministry in The Early Church._ Fortress Press, 1989, . 13.
3 Ibid

4 Ibid.
5 Thurston, *The Widows,* Fortress Press, 1989, p. 16.
6 Gillian Clark, *Women in Late Antiquity*, Clarendon Press, Oxford, England, 1993, pp. 46–51.
7 Ibid.

CHAPTER 8

1 Neil Clark Warren, Interview with *Single Adult Ministry Journal,* "The Idolatry of Marriage," Issue 110, May 1995.
2 Interview with Dr. Dennis Guernsey, *Single Adult Ministry Journal,* Vol. 10, Issue 95, 1992, pp. 8–10.

CHAPTER 9

1 Assuming 2.5 members in over 11 million single parent families.
2 David Gyertson, *Good News*, "Ministry in the New Millennium," September, 1998, pp. 12–16.
3 Gillian Clark, p. 51. Taken from *Homily 66 on Matthew 3*, PG 58.630.
4 Howard Clark Kee and Franklin Young, *Understanding the New Testament,* Prentice Hall, 1957, p. 356.
5 Lynda Hunter, "The Cutting Edge," Single Parent Family Magazine, January 1998, p. 4.

CHAPTER 11

1 Interview with Lindsey Erwin, Woman at the Well Ministry, Woodland Park, CO., May 1997.

CHAPTER 12

1 Nick Stinnett and John DeFrain, *Secrets of Strong Families,* Berkley Books, New York, N.Y., 1986.

To order additonal copies of

The
Hidden
Mission
Field

send $12.95 plus $4.95 shipping and handling to

Books, Etc.
PO Box 1406
Mukilteo, WA 98275

or have your credit card ready and call

(800) 917-BOOK